Autism Grows Up

Book 5 of the School Daze Series

Dr. Sharon A. Mitchell

This is a work of fiction, a figment of the author's imagination. Any resemblance to real people or events is coincidental. This story is for entertainment and information purposes only. The author assumes no responsibility for the strategies or suggestions described.

Copyright © 2016 Sharon A. Mitchell

All rights reserved.

ISBN: 198842304X
ISBN-13: 978-1-988423-04-3

TO SHAWN

Who has not let fear stand in his way of experiencing life.

Other books in the School Daze Series:

Autism Goes to School

Autism Runs Away

Autism Belongs

Autism Talks & Talks

Autism Grows Up

The Autism Goes to School Workbook (coming in 2017)

Prequel to Autism Goes to School (coming in 2017)

Contents

PROLOGUE 1

CHAPTER 1 5

CHAPTER 2 9

CHAPTER 3 14

CHAPTER 4 21

CHAPTER 5 26

CHAPTER 6 32

CHAPTER 7 38

CHAPTER 8 45

CHAPTER 9 51

CHAPTER 10 61

CHAPTER 11 66

CHAPTER 12 75

CHAPTER 13 87

Other Books in the Series 104

Autism Goes to School 105

What Are Reviewers Saying About Autism Goes to School? 106

Autism Runs Away 107

Autism Belongs 108

Autism Talks and Talks	109
Autism Grows Up	110
Autism Goes to School Workbook	112
Prequel to Autism Goes to School	113
ABOUT THE AUTHOR	114

GRATITUDE GALORE

This book owes a huge debt to the wonderful editors who offered their wisdom, and critical eyes to this work - Andi, Ellen, Lynn, Mary, Michelle and Penny.

PROLOGUE

There it was again, that creak. Her eye, the one not snuggled into the pillow, opened. Somehow, it was easier to listen with her eye open. Now, how did that work? She lifted her head slightly off the down pillow so she could hear with both ears.

Snick. Her head popped up. She held her neck crooked at an uncomfortable angle as her eyes tried to peer through the darkness. She knew that sound. That scraping noise came when a knife was withdrawn from the knife block on the counter. The largest butcher knife, in fact. Now what in the world would Suzie be doing with that knife?

There was a creak. Yep, the floor in front of the dishwasher. The butcher block lived on the counter by the dishwasher. But, it took a lot of weight to make that particular spot creak. Even Amanda herself didn't cause the floor to protest. Her dad and her brother, yes, and Cousin Sylvia who was pushing 250, yes. But not Suzie, who was barely one hundred ten pounds after being caught out in a rain deluge.

The footsteps were coming this way, not that there were many places to go in this house. Amanda grabbed the quilt and sheet carefully in one hand and slowly drew back the covers as silently as she could. For once she was grateful that she was unable to afford that soft, down duvet she'd so admired. Rubbing it with her hands in the Bed 'n Bath store, she'd known the noise it would make every time she turned over in bed. What did that matter though when you slept alone and it didn't look like that would ever change. Thankful that she had a king-sized quilt on her queen-sized bed, Amanda bumped up the quilt in the middle of the bed, hoping it might look like a body slept soundly there. Glancing at the rocker in the corner, she remembered Chatty Cathy, the doll of her childhood, the doll who stood nearly as tall as her six year old self at the time. Cathy had long hair. Maybe, just maybe, if she tucked her into the bed, Cathy would pass for a slumbering human.

A shoe scraped on the bathroom linoleum tile. His foot must have caught on that spot in front of the sink where the tile's lifting. His? Of course it was a his. Who ever heard of a woman breaking into someone's house?

Hide. She had what, maybe three seconds before he made it this way. Her head swiveled, eyes scanning for the likely spots. She snatched up the mini-led flashlight she kept by her bed. Its light was intense and she had bought it for its weight and compact size. Now, she wished for the days when she had that bulky, long flashlight that resembled a billy club.

She lay on her stomach and inched her feet under the bed. That worked until her hips reached the edge. No go. She eased out again and flipped over onto her back. Wiggling back under, she used her elbows for purchase. This time when her hips stuck, she braced her upper arms on the floor and lifted the edge of the box spring with her hands. Only the edge of mattress was firm, she remembered. The inside was covered by just some flimsy material that had already torn when she'd gotten the vacuum nozzle stuck there some years ago. Thank god for the carpet to dull the noises she was making.

Turning her head to the side, she was under. The dust under here was incredible. When had she last vacuumed? Sure, she stuck the nozzle under here every week. Well, every few weeks, but had she ever actually moved the bed to give a good cleaning? This coming weekend, she promised herself. Yes, she would live through this and become a better housekeeper.

Her ears picked up the tiny sound of her doorknob rotating in its cylinder. She turned her head. Softly, slowly, the door gently scraped the carpet in a wide arc. Amanda could see the edges of scruffy Nikes with the emblem on the side.

Pushing her cheek into the floor more, she glimpsed his silhouette as he advanced into the room. The glow from the moonlight coming in her open curtains helped. Or, not. The sheen glinted off the upheld butcher knife, the one kept so shiny and fine-edged by the built-in sharpener. Amanda's eyes closed and her lips sealed against that tiny whimper that wanted to escape.

Tap, tap, tap. A pause, then, tap-tap, tap-tap as his steps stopped. His Nikes swiveled in place, aiming towards her bed, lingering, then moving toward the window. The tapping stopped.

Slowly, slowly, the scuffed shoes turned. They turned her way. The tap, tap resumed. Was he peering at the bed? Estimating the size and shape of her body? The best place to strike first?

Every nerve in her body seized. Petrified wood had nothing on her. She willed even the blood in her veins to hold still. His toes pointed her way.

Faintly, then more and more discernible, the tapping resumed. Along with it came a humming. The sound was low, almost more a growl than anything melodious. Was he trying to hum a tune? Good grief, a tone-deaf assailant. Amanda winced. What was wrong with her brain? At a time like this, she'd criticize someone's musical ability?

"Come out, come out, wherever you are." Then a low growl. There was a tearing sound as his knife, really her knife, raked at the clothes. Her good clothes. Did he have any idea how many hours she had spent scouring the second hand stores to acquire such a decent wardrobe? No one at work ever guessed where she got her outfits. Now, they were being ruined.

Amanda felt something else stirring in her gut. This time, it went beyond resentment. How dare he? How dare this stranger enter her home, terrorize her, then destroy her clothing? Her fists tightened against her side; her toes clenched. She was powerless to defend herself, defend her home. Why, oh why, had she chosen to cower under the bed? She was wedged like a gherkin in a sealed jar. It would take her minutes to worm her way out, then what?

The sound of his escalated breathing penetrated Amanda's brain. It was rapid, noisy and wheezy, as if fragments of her tattered, knifed clothing had floated up his nose, clogging his sinuses. Good, let him suffocate himself. Death by polyester and flame retardants.

Her thoughts were like herded cats, scattering, going their own way, with no cohesiveness at the time when she needed it most. Think Amanda, think. What will you do when he checks under the bed?

Her clenching fingers brushed something chilly and firm. The giddy part of her mind assured her that no part of her body was firm, so it must be something else. She scrunched one shoulder lower to lengthen her reach. There, her fingers brushed it again. Slithering an inch farther, her baby finger snagged it. Her flashlight. Her four-inch long, LED flashlight. Well, it shone brightly, so maybe she could flick it into his eyes, momentarily blinding him while she made a dash to get out from under the bed. Dash. Right. If she made it from under the bed, then she'd be parrying his knife thrusts with her mighty four inch flashlight.

His breathing, if anything, was heavier now. The knife no longer slashed, but beat against his pant leg as he returned to her bed.

The humming was replaced by grunts. Low, guttural, pigs-at-the-trough-like grunts. What was he doing? Punching her bed? Did he not know she wasn't there? Why punch the covers? Feathers floated along the edge of the bed, sprinkling the carpet with down. The knife. He was slashing her bed with her butcher knife.

Amanda shivered. She knew his intent. She'd have to act fast, catch him by surprise. Surely she could get out from under the bed fast. There was no need for stealth and she knew that she'd need to lift it off herself. She did it once, she could do it again when her life and that of Suzie's depended on it.

The slashing punches stopped. The toes remained pointed towards her while his breath heaved. Knifing a bed must be hard work, Amanda's errant brain decided.

Was his breathing slowing just a little? Amanda felt that she could hear his heart beating, her senses were so acute. He took a shuffling step back from the bed. One knee pressed to the carpet. Then, the hand with the knife rested on the floor near the edge of the bed. Should she try to make a grab for it? No, too far. She'd eased herself to the side farthest from him. Plus, what good would grabbing the blade do?

Now his forearm rested on the floor as well. She could see the sweat-stained pits of his raggedy shirt. Her nose registered his b.o., even over top of the perfume. Then one eye, a nose, mouth and part of a second eye peered at her. His lips formed something that might be mistaken for a grin if you were one of the walking dead.

"Hello," his gravelly voice said. "Ready for some fun?"

CHAPTER 1

Amanda pulled into the driveway and observed her darkened house. Would it be too much to ask that there be a few lights on? Maybe the outside light so she could see to put her key in the lock. Maybe the kitchen light or the table lamp beside the couch? A cheery glow through the drapes would be nice. And, what if she opened the door only to be welcomed by the smell of freshly baked bread, or lasagna bubbling in the oven? Even a can of tomato soup warming on the stove would be great. But no, that didn't happen in her house. She rested her head on the steering wheel.

The chill from the damp, evening air entered her bones. It had drizzled on and off most of the afternoon. How long had she sat there? No, there was no change in the house's facade, no twitching curtain, no door opening to see where she was. And there likely would not be.

Slowly, stiffly, Amanda got out of the car. She pushed the button to pop the trunk, then balancing carefully, she managed to gather up each and every grocery bag. She hated making more than one trip and heaven knew there would be no offers to bring in the food for her.

Juggling her bags to get the key in the lock wasn't working. Instead, Amanda rang the bell. Surely Suzie would hear and come open the door for her. She waited. And waited. Rang the doorbell again. Harder. She pounded with her toe, but her suede boot was no louder than the bell. Nope, Suzie was likely in the basement, as usual, and would be oblivious to the rest of the world.

Amanda struggled to rearrange her burdens. The handle of one of the plastic bags tore, unbalancing that load and part of a bag of apples bounced onto the cracked pavement, then into the flower beds. She gave up and unwound her hands from the plastic handles, setting half of her load on the still wet concrete. She got the door opened, stepped in with what was in her hands and deposited the dry bags on the counter. "Suzie," she called. She returned for the rest of the groceries, placing the dirty bags on the floor. "Suzie, wanna come give me a hand?" There was no answer.

Sighing, Amanda began putting away the food. There was no point in making an issue about Suzie helping her. Been there, done that. And, look where it had got her. How had they come to this?

Quit whining, she told herself. This is just the way it is. When you have a kid who is different, you have to expect a different kind of life. But, this was not what she had signed on for.

Then the other part, the mother part of her brain kicked in. It was not Suzie's fault that she had been born like this. She stepped to the beat of her own drummer and Amanda admired that in her daughter. Suzie had the courage to go her own way and was not influenced by peer pressure. Amanda might be feeling sorry for herself right this minute, but she had escaped all those years of teenage angst and drama and worry other parents talk about.

And, Suzie was smart - brilliant, probably, or at least Amanda thought so. She smiled. What mother didn't think she had birthed a genius or at least a remarkable child?

Soon, the aromas of heated garlic bread, garlicky Caesar salad, and carrot soup filled the air, raising Amanda's spirits. Thank goodness for deli counters in the supermarkets. And the fact that they served dishes Suzie could tolerate.

"Suzie," she called. No answer. Opening the door to the basement, she tried again. "Suzie, it's time to set the table. Supper's almost ready." She waited. "Now".

"In a minute, mom."

"Now. I've been home half an hour. You know you're supposed to have this done before I get here."

"In a minute. I'm just at an important part. I've almost made the next level."

Amanda gritted her teeth. How she hated those computer games that engulfed so much of Suzie's time. Whoever invented such things was definitely not a mother. They were an addiction with kids these days.

In the back of her mind she heard that little voice remind her, "We get the children we raise." Of course, that didn't apply to her though. Her child was different, was born different. Suzie couldn't help it and she couldn't be expected to do the things that came so easily to others her age.

Turning, Amanda opened the drawer by the table and withdrew two placemats. Then, she laid out the cutlery, plates and bowls. She put the croutons in the bowl with the duckies, the one Suzie had so loved as a child.

"Supper," she yelled down. "Come now, while it's hot."

After pouring the bubbling, fragrant soup into their bowls, she washed out the pot, wiped off the stove and tidied the counter. She thought about hunting in the juniper bush for the lost apples, but decided to leave that until daylight. Maybe Suzie could do that tomorrow.

Amanda sat down and dipped a spoon into her soup. A swirl of sour cream would go nicely with the pale orange of the soup. She spooned some into a measuring cup and heated it in the microwave. She then poured the warmed cream into a pleasing pattern in their soup bowls.

Where was Suzie? Stupid question. Of course, she knew where she was - plastered in front of her computer. As always. Should she start without her? Make an issue of it? It seemed that she was always trying to pick her battles, always weighing if it was worth starting a row.

She was the mother, right? Right. What did it matter that her kid was legally an adult, actually way past the age of consent and reason. If Suzie acted like a child, she should be treated like a child. Right? Oh, how Amanda wished she had a partner to help with these decisions, someone with whom she could share the responsibility.

Amanda straightened. Well, she didn't have a partner, and she hadn't had anyone for a long time. It had been just her and Suzie and it looked like it would always be the two of them.

"Suzie!" It wasn't often that Amanda yelled, but this time it was a righteous yell. "Suzie, get up here right now!"

"But Mom, I'm almost at the end of level five. It's taken me forever to reach this. If I stop now...."

"I don't care. You get your butt up here right now." She added, "Or else."

Suzie knew what "or else" meant. She'd experienced it - not often, but the few occasions had been too much. Her mom had cut off her computer access.

Minutes later, her steps dragging, Suzie entered the kitchen. She fell into her chair, slouching, with arms crossed. The wafting smells of the now cooling carrot curry soup didn't move her. The geometric swirls of warmed sour cream decorating her soup bowl didn't register. Her body screamed *I'm here but you can't make me like it.*

True, true, all too true. But as the responsible adult, Amanda could set a few rules. Oh, but how much easier life would be if she didn't have to. Suck it up, buttercup. This is the hand you've been dealt. Live it.

Taking the high road, Amanda decided to ignore the petulant adolescent attitude sitting in front of her. Just act natural. Pretend like this was any mother-adult-daughter situation.

"You'll never believe the day I've had," she started. Was Suzie listening? Did she even care? Amanda described an outrageous call she'd had. She talked about the antics of the mail delivery guy, a wanna-be stand-up comedian, who entertained them daily. She talked as if she had an appreciative audience, sipping soup in between anecdotes, hoping, so hoping for a two-way conversation.

Gradually, Suzie's arms unfolded and she picked up her spoon. Never a word about how good the food tasted, or how attractive the garnishes were, but still, she ate and without too much fuss. Amanda reminded herself to be grateful for small mercies.

Despite the fact that Amanda did all the talking, she still finished her meal ahead of her daughter. Suzie ate slowly. Always. She'd take a bite then seem to roll it around in her mouth rather than just chew and swallow. The chewing she did do was thorough and methodical. She inspected morsels before putting them into her mouth; she didn't like surprises with her food. And, she'd get none tonight. There was nothing too hot, too spicy nor too crunchy, all deal-breakers when it came to Suzy and eating. Amanda had made sure that the cos lettuce used in the salad had the firmer ribs removed and the lettuce was cut into small, bite-sized pieces that would not overcrowd Suzie's sensitive mouth. She remembered cutting the crusts off Suzie's bread, and cooling off food to just the right temperature before the toddler would tolerate any food. And, different foods could not touch each other on the plate. Back then, white and brown foods were okay, but nothing green or orange. Thank goodness that phase was over and they could have vegetables with their meals.

"Come on, Suzie. Get a move on. We have plans for this evening."

Suzie paused with her fork partway to her mouth. Amanda cursed her timing. Now, it would take time for Suzie to get back into the motion of eating.

Amanda reached under the table where she'd stashed the Scrabble board. "I plan to wipe my daughter off the board this evening. I feel it in my bones that tonight's my night."

"Mom, you haven't beaten me at Scrabble since I was nine."

"I'm quite sure you're not right about that."

"No, I was nine, a little over nine since my birthday was the month before that game. You won because I drew lousy letters and had no vowels for most of the game."

"How can you remember such things?"

"I remember everything."

"Well, remember to shovel down that food while I get the board set up."

CHAPTER 2

"That's thirty-three with the triple word score." Suzie marked down her score, comparing it to her mother's lagging performance.

"How do you do that?" asked Amanda.

"You go with what you're given and play the best game you can."

"That's what I do and it doesn't work for me. Obviously."

"Never give up. When you're stumped, mix things up and look at it another way. There's always a way; it just might look different than you thought it might. You might have a different spin on it, but you can still be a winner."

Her words slowly sunk into Amanda's consciousness. Suzie might be talking about Scrabble, but did she realize what she'd said? Was she referring to her life?

Whether she meant it that way or not, still, it brought meaning to Suzie's existence. Or could.

Amanda had been so hopeful when she first held Suzie in her arms. Her beautiful, dark-haired delight. Even though those toddler and preschool years were tough, Amanda's hope returned when they realized how gifted Suzie was academically. She whizzed through the grades, barely studying, never being side-tracked by the teenage angst or social triumphs and disasters that floated around her. High school was rough with the bullying and teasing, but once that was over, life should get better for her daughter. Or so she had thought. Instead, life stopped, just stopped for Suzie once she finished grade 12.

Never give up, Suzie just said. But wasn't that what she had done?

You go with what you're given and play the best game you can. What Suzie had been given was a mixture of blessings, talents and challenges. Was she doing the best she could with what she'd been given. Was lurking in the basement, engrossed in games and hobbies of her choice the best she could do? If this was her best and as good as it would get for Suzie, was she, as her mother, doing what she should to support her? But what if this was not the best Suzie could do? Could she do more? If so, what did she need from Amanda to get to her best?

The phone rang during Amanda's turn. "Get that, will you please, Suzie."

There was no movement. Amanda looked up at her daughter. "Suzie, please."

"You know I don't like to answer the phone. How do I know who it is?"

"We had caller ID installed because of that. Remember? We pay extra to have the service so you won't have that problem."

"But not every number comes up. And what if the person asks me something I don't know?"

Amanda got up to catch the phone on its fifth ring. She sighed then schooled her features to a neutral expression so her exasperation wouldn't show in her voice. "Hello."

She listened, and then her face brightened. "Sure. We're just sitting here playing Scrabble and I'm getting my butt whipped." She waited. "Yes, again. I know, I know. Come on over. We'll be waiting."

She returned to her seat and peered at the seven letters resting on her wooden stand. "That was Uncle Todd. He says he's two stoplights away and coming over with an ice cream pie and a bottle of wine."

Suzie gave no indication that she'd heard.

When the knock came, it was again Amanda's turn at the board. "Go get the door, Suzie. You know who it is."

As Suzie approached the door, her mom reminded her, "But check through the peep hole before you open the door to make sure it really is Uncle Todd."

Todd brought the damp, chilly air in with hm. One hand clutched a paper sack and the other grasped the neck of a bottle. He wrapped that arm around Suzie and pulled her in snuggly to his side. "Hello there, youngun'. Great to see ya." As Suzie started to struggle away, he wrapped her tighter. "I know you don't like to be touched. But humor your old uncle. I don't get to see you every day and I'm squeezing hard the way you told me to."

Suzie's arms wound around her uncle and pressed for just a second. He released an arm and ruffled her hair. "How's my favorite niece?"

"Uncle Todd. I'm your only niece. I've told you that before."

"And, I've told you that you're my favorite." He set his bottle of wine and the ice cream pie on the table. "Go grab us some plates, Suzie and let's have this dessert."

Suzie hesitated in front of the cupboards.

"And bring a knife to cut it and some forks, too."

She got what she needed from the cutlery drawer, and then opened two cupboard doors before she found the right one. Amanda wondered if her daughter actually didn't know where they kept the dessert plates.

"Your mom sent out a distress signal. She told me she was being massacred once again by her loving daughter and needed reinforcements."

Suzie looked at her mom. "I didn't see you making any calls."

"Todd," Amanda reproached. "I've told you not to tease Suzie. She doesn't like it."

"Who does?" he asked. "That's why it's called teasing. She doesn't mind it from me, do you Suzie Q?"

"Not the teasing so much, but you know that I hate being called Suzie Q. I'm not three anymore."

"Nope, you couldn't wump your mother at Scrabble when you were three." He pulled Amanda's tiles over so he could have a look. "Let's see what we can do with this mess. With your mom and I teaming against you, this should now be a fair fight."

Well, it wasn't. Suzie still won not just that game, but the next one as well when they each played their own tiles.

Todd leaned back and stretched. "Well, that was enough brain work for me for one night. Come Amanda. Let's relax in the living room and crack open this bottle of wine." He stood up. "Suzie, do you want to join us after you've cleaned up the kitchen?"

Suzie stood with one hand on the basement door. "I've got a lot of stuff to get done. I think I'll say good night."

Amanda stood to clear their dessert dishes off the table.

Todd placed a hand on Amanda's arm to still her, then took the plates from her hands and replaced them on the table.

"Wait," he said. Suzie took two steps down the stairs. "Wait," he said louder. His voice was firm. Suzie turned to look at him.

"Suzie, who cooked supper?"

Puzzled, Suzie answered, "Mom did."

"Who set the table?"

"Mom. I was busy."

"Who was away at work all day?"

"Mom was at her job. I was doing some of my work too."

Todd wiped a hand down his face as his eyes rolled toward his brows. "Here's the thing, Suzie. Whoever makes supper gets to sit and relax afterward. Whoever benefits from that supper without working on it gets to clean up. That's how it works. One person makes supper, the other cleans up. And, cleans up well."

Suzie's rebellious look showed. Sensing a tantrum brewing, Amanda stepped in.

"It's fine, Todd. I'm not that tired and there's really not that much to do. Suzie wants to get back to her computer." Noticing her brother's look, she added. "Really, it's okay."

Sensing a reprieve, Suzie's shoulders relaxed and she turned to go down another step.

"No, it is not okay." Todd's voice was steel. "Suzie, get back up here and do your part. Your mother and I are going to enjoy a glass of wine while you make this kitchen tidy and spotless. Then, if you want, we'd love to have you join us."

Taking Amanda's arm in one hand, he juggled the bottle, two glasses and an opener in the other. When Amanda dragged her feet and would have said more, he gave her a glare and pulled her along.

Once in the living room, Amanda rounded on her brother. "Now, you've upset her."

"Oh, give me a break, Amanda. Can't you see what you're doing?"

"When you have kids, you can criticize my parenting. Until then, butt out."

"No such luck. Can't you see that little Suzie is taking advantage of you? And that little Suzie isn't exactly little anymore. She's what? Twenty?"

"Twenty-one."

"What were you doing when you were twenty-one?"

"Likely I was changing Suzie's diapers. It seemed like that's about all I did for a couple years."

"Yeah, that kid was a handful and you did most of the heavy lifting on your own. I admired you for that and did for years and years, but not so much now."

"What do you mean? I'm still looking after my daughter."

"Yes, you are. But, should you be? I know. I know she's different and that some things are tougher for her. But dishes? Would it kill her to clear the table and put the dirty stuff in the dishwasher?"

"She does. Sometimes."

Todd looked skeptical. "There are two of you living here but as far as I can see, only one of you does all the work."

"You know how hard Suzie finds it to go out on her own. Having a job right now is too much to ask of her."

"Maybe it is just at this present time, but are you going to live like this forever?"

"She just needs more time."

"Mandy, she's been out of high school for over three years. How much more time does she need?"

Amanda shrugged. Todd was right that things did not seem to be getting easier for her daughter. That urge to move out on her own and get on with her life didn't seem to have taken root in Suzie as it did in most teens. But she didn't know what to do, how to help her little girl.

Todd's exasperation had turned to sympathy. He squeezed his big sister's hand. In the other room, cutlery was flung into the rack in the dishwasher. Plates were stacked together, likely harder than was necessary. For a hundred and five pound little woman, Suzie could sure stomp.

Todd tried again. "Maybe she's not ready to enter the job market tomorrow. But there are things you can do to help bolster her confidence."

Amanda glared. "I'm good for Suzie's self-esteem. I'm always finding ways to praise her and point out her strengths."

"I know you are. That's not what I mean, though. You gain confidence by doing things. Taking on responsibilities. Thinking of someone other than yourself. Participating in your own care and that of others."

As Amanda started to protest, Todd held up his hand. "Just listen for a minute, will you? You work hard all day. You need this job to support the two of you and keep this house running. Suzie's not going to be contributing financially any day soon. But, she can contribute in other ways. What's so wrong about having a rule that you cook and she cleans up? Or, better yet, why should you not come home each day to a meal already made? Suzie's home all day long; couldn't she be in charge of cooking supper?"

"I can just imagine what kind of a meal we'd have. Left-over ramen noodles with grated cheese. Frozen fries heated in the oven. A bowl of cereal."

"Mandy, whose fault is that? How do other people learn to cook? Do their mothers teach them? Does someone insist that they read a recipe book or look something up online then follow the cooking directions?"

"Todd, I get what you're saying. I'm just so tired is all and most of the time I'm just not up for a fight."

"Why should...." Todd began, when the phone rang. "Let her get it," he suggested.

"No, she hates answering the phone."

CHAPTER 3

Amanda grabbed the cordless extension off the end table. "Hello?" She listened for a second, then her face reddened and she turned away, walking toward the hall. She turned back and raised one finger to Todd. She'd just be a minute.

Todd put his feet up on the coffee table and grabbed the remote. He hit mute while he channel surfed, looking for something good.

Amanda's voice dropped lower, with a quality he had not heard in a long time. What was that? There it was again. Was it, really? Yes, Amanda giggled. There, she did it again. How many years had it been since he'd seen Amanda act like a carefree girl? Who was she talking to?

Her voice got quieter and Todd could barely make out her murmurs. Tiring of the ads, he decided to help himself to one more piece of ice cream cake during the commercial break. He passed Amanda in the hallway. She stood with her shoulders resting on the wall, head back and one foot resting on the toe of her shoe. When she spied Todd, she half-turned away. He squeezed her shoulder as he went by.

As he got his plate from the cupboard and opened the freezer, he could hear her part of the conversation.

"No, I couldn't possibly," he heard Amanda saying. "I have a..." there was a hesitation, "situation at home. I couldn't Saturday. Or any night. I'm not really free in the evenings."

Todd stopped clattering dishes and listened. Was he hearing what he thought he was hearing? Did his sister have an opportunity to go out, maybe do something with friends and she was turning it down? Because of Suzie? Why else?

He pushed by Amanda, giving her a stern look as he went. He opened the basement door and called down the stairs. "Suzie, I'll be back Saturday evening for a rematch. Just you and me this time. Without your mom's pestering, I'll wipe the board with your tiles."

"You're on, Uncle Todd."

There. Was that loud enough? Todd hoped whoever was on the other end of that phone line had heard and knew now that Amanda would indeed be free Saturday because he'd be here with Suzie.

Taking his ice cream back to the living room, he got a scowl from Amanda. After a few more minutes, he heard her say another "sorry', then hang up.

Amanda came into the living room, sat in the arm chair and pretended to be engrossed in paper towel endurance tests on the television.

Todd scooped several more bites into his mouth, waiting. "Well?" he finally asked.

"Well what?"

"Sis." He gave her a disgusted look. "Who was that?"

"Just someone from work."

"A call about work?"

"Sort of. Yeah, about work."

"Mandy, you were a lousy liar as a kid and your skills have not improved with time. Give. Who was that?"

"A salesman who comes to the office."

"What, he forgot his briefcase? His phone? What did he want?"

Amanda shook her head. "No, he didn't forget anything. I think he just wanted to talk."

"To you?"

"Yes, to me. Geez. Some people do like to talk to me, you know." She threw him a look. "You were a jerk as a kid and you haven't improved on that with time."

"Yeah, yeah, yeah. I'm your brother - that's my job. Tell me more about this guy. What's his name? How'd you meet him? Why's he calling you at home?"

Amanda sighed. "You're not going to leave this alone, are you?"

Todd shook his head.

"His name's Jack Fleming. He's a salesman we deal with. It used to be infrequent, more of a fill-in thing, but he's been transferred to this area recently, so he's the rep I deal with through our orders. And, since he's new to this city, he doesn't know a lot of people, other than those he's met through his job. So, he's called a couple times to chat."

Todd tilted his head and looked at her, holding the spoon sticking out the side of his mouth. He made a circling motion with the index finger of his other hand.

Her brother was determined to be a pain about this, so, she humored him. Actually, the more she talked about Jack, the easier it got. She couldn't see her posture relax or her face become more animated. But, Todd did.

"So what was that about you having a situation at home?" He waved his spoon around the living room. "Everything here looks okay to me and Suzie even cleaned up the kitchen all right. What's this situation you're supposed to have?"

"Situation wasn't really the right word, I guess, but I didn't want to get into personal stuff with Jack. He might not understand."

He took his feet off the coffee table and straightened up. "Personal stuff? Are you sick?"

"No, you idiot. I mean with Suzie. I didn't want to tell Jack that I have an adult daughter with, you know."

"How old does this guy think you are? Too young to have a kid Suzie's age? How old is he?"

"Not sure, but I'd say he's about my age, maybe a bit older. Mid-forties or so. He's a widower, with no children. Anyone can tell my age. Despite that, he seems interested in me." Amanda straightened and she covered her lips with two fingers. Too late; it was out.

"Huh! Now we're getting somewhere. So, he's interested in you, is he? Well, the guy sounds all right so far, and you sound interested in him. So what's the problem? Why aren't you going out?"

Amanda gave him an exasperated look. "Geez, Todd, you are dense." She jerked her head toward the cellar stairs.

"You've got a crick in your neck?"

Amanda threw the chair pillow at him.

Todd tried again. "You can't get a babysitter?"

"To-od."

"No, seriously. What's the problem?"

"Suzie. You know I can't leave her alone."

"Why not? You do when you go to work every day."

"I know and I feel badly enough about that. She's alone so much of the time already."

"So, she has her life; you have yours. That's the way things are."

"No, not really. Suzie doesn't have a life. She's in that basement alone, plugged in to the computer. The only human contact she has, the only interaction with another human beings is when I'm here."

Todd raised both eyebrows and brought his thumbs up to point at his own chest.

"Or, when you come over," Amanda amended. "She loves your visits. You help a lot, thanks. I guess I don't say that enough, but I truly am grateful for your presence in our lives."

Todd grinned and mimed taking out a pen and notebook. "Can I write that down? Save it for posterity?"

"I wish I had something left to throw at you. Give you a compliment and it goes to your head."

"Seriously, Sis, why are you and this Jack guy not going out?"

Amanda just looked at him. That look their mother would give him when she was tired of reminding him to take out the garbage.

"Not this Suzie business again? Are you hiding behind your daughter? Shame on you, Amanda May."

"No, I'm not hiding behind anyone. Or, anything. It's just too difficult. If Suzie was your typical twenty-one year old, it would be different, but she's not. She's just not. She needs me."

"Yeah. She needs you to cook her meals and do the dishes and the laundry and clean up after her."

"Todd, it's not like that and you know it. You can pretend all you want that Asperger's Syndrome doesn't affect her life, but I know better."

"Mandy, look, I know. I get it that she has Asperger's. But Asperger's is not a death sentence – for her or for you. I read the same books you do but I get different things out of them. I see Asperger's as a way of looking at the world differently, but you see it as a series of 'I can'ts'."

Amanda started to protest but Todd held up his hand.

"You do. You see having Asperger's as an excuse to retreat from the world. And not just that, as an excuse to be self-indulgent."

"You have no idea what you're talking about. You don't live here. You don't see her in the throes of an anxiety attack. You have no idea what it's like." Amanda stood up. "I'm going to bed. You can see yourself out."

Todd licked his spoon, returning his feet to the coffee table. To himself, he mused, "In some hinky way, I think we may have made a little progress." He manned the remote.

Amanda fumed. Her brother could really get on her nerves sometimes. Too bad he was her only sibling. It would be nice to have some other brothers or sisters to hang out with. Less annoying ones. Less opinionated ones. He had no idea what life was like with Suzie, the struggles she went through and all that Amanda had to put up with. Did he think she liked playing maid for an adult daughter? Did he think she didn't wish she could wave a magic wand and make Suzie have the kind of life other girls her age considered normal and their right? A tear trailed down her cheek, burying itself with its sisters in her pillow. She flipped the pillow over, seeking a cooler, drier spot.

Their fight had started because of that phone call from Jack. Jack. He'd been calling more often lately and it was nice to talk to him, to have some adult conversation without controversy or nagging or treading on eggshells.

Jack was all right; she loved their phone chats and, when they talked at the office. What would it be like to go on an actual date? Maybe have dinner together? Go for a walk? Anything. Just to get away for a little while and forget that she was a mother with a big responsibility. What if she could just be Amanda?

Could she? What would Suzie think?

Ridiculous. Of course, she couldn't. Suzie came first; she was her mother. She'd birthed Suzie and took full responsibility for her. Gladly. Still....

Her phone was wedged between her cheek and shoulder, one hand marked her place on a page and the fingers of her other hand worked the keyboard. There was another call parked in call waiting, she had four messages she'd not yet returned this morning, she'd not even checked her email messages and she was a mess.

It was Todd's fault. She'd had a lousy night, tossing and thinking and what-iffing all night long. She'd even heard Suzie come to bed around three-thirty. Usually she was dead asleep by then, thanks to her ear plugs and exhaustion. But no, because of Todd's interference and innuendos and butting in, she'd hardly slept. Then she woke up late, sleeping through the alarm and not having time for her shower. As a result, her hair was total bed head.

Someone called her name. She lowered her chin and raised her eyes to peer over her reading glasses.

Great, just great. Jack was here, standing in front of her desk with that smile, that smile that warmed her to her toes, that smile that made her feel like her presence warmed his day. Drats. She looked such a wreck today. Would it be too uncool to slide these papers up in front of her face? Or pretend she dropped something then crawl under her desk and stay there until he went away?

Jack's grin, that same one he always gave her, seemed to slip. "Amanda, are you all right?"

She nodded.

"Am I interrupting you? Of course I am. I can see that you're doing three things at once. I just wanted to see you, to talk to you again." He looked around to see if her co-workers were paying attention. "I enjoyed our conversation last night."

Amanda nodded. Idiot, she thought. Did that nod mean she was agreeing that he'd enjoyed talking to her? She found her voice. "I enjoyed it to."

Jack cleared his throat. "There was something I wanted to ask you."

Oh no, thought Amanda. Please, please don't. Let's just continue on the way we are. It's pleasant. And safe.

"About what I suggested last night. I really would like to go out for dinner with you. Or to a show or a play, or something. Anything. Just to talk to you, spend some time with you away from work."

When Amanda hesitated, he added, "You can pick the time and place. Whatever you'd like I know I'll enjoy."

He really was a nice man, but how to explain? "Jack, thank you for the invitation. In other circumstances I'd love to go out with you, but I can't. I have responsibilities at home and I need to be there."

"What responsibilities do you have that you can't get away for just a couple hours? We would not have to be out late if you don't want."

Amanda just looked at him, at a loss for what to say, how to explain without painting either herself or her daughter in a bad light. Why should it matter what this man thought? He was nothing to her, to them. But, somehow it did matter.

"Do you have elder care? A dog? Small children?" Then another look crossed his face and he straightened then took a step back. "Are you married?"

"Hmph, nothing like that. I mean, I was married, once a long time ago, but he left us almost twenty years ago."

"Us?"

"My daughter and myself."

"Would your daughter like to come out with us? I like kids? We could go for pizza if she'd prefer that."

Yes, he definitely was a nice man. "Yes, Suzie does like pizza, but she doesn't like going out much. She's pretty much a home-body."

"Then how about I come over and bring pizza? And beer or wine or chocolate milk. How old is Suzie?"

Here it comes. He'll never understand. "Twenty-one."

"Oh." There was silence. "I'm not sure I follow. If she's twenty-one, can't she stay home alone? Doesn't she go out herself?"

"My daughter is different." She lowered her voice. No one at work knew about her personal life. "Suzie has a condition - it's called Asperger's Syndrome, a form of high-functioning autism. It makes life hard for her. She doesn't get people and avoids socializing with anyone except me and maybe a couple of close family members."

"Does she have friends?"

Amanda shook her head. "No, not really. She says she has some friends, but they're people she's never actually met - online friends, mostly in gaming sites or some online autism support groups. Other than that...."

"Is she able to be at home alone during the day while you're at work? Does she attend some sort of sheltered workshop when you're away?"

Amanda's back stiffened. "She has Asperger's, not an intellectual disability. She's smart, really smart. She just has social problems. And anxiety." She waited to see if Jack would draw the conclusion that her daughter was nuts. The public had strange ideas about mental illness and Suzie's degree of anxiety seemed to indeed make her unstable.

"Will she get better?"

Good question. Amanda shook her head. "I'd like to think so, but I'm not sure. I rather doubt it. Over the last few years, things seem to have gotten worse."

"I'm not a scary guy, honest. Maybe if she gradually got used to a few more people...What about if I come over on the weekend? I could bring pizza, like I said. Maybe we could go for a walk, or watch a movie or make popcorn."

Amanda shook her head.

"What would she do if I dropped by?"

"Probably hide in the basement."

"What would she be doing anyway?"

What could she say? Hide in the basement? How would that sound to Jack? Amanda looked at him standing, so earnest, so willing to fit in, so normal. What would it be like to have a man like this as her friend, in her life? What would it be like for Suzie? No, she's seen how Suzie reacted to strangers before. A brief stop at the supermarket was agonizing for her. No, Suzie was her responsibility and her child must come first. As much as she might like to see where a relationship could go with this man, it would be kinder to both of them to cut it off here.

CHAPTER 4

Return home, deja vu, thought Amanda. Again, it was a damp evening. Again, she had sacks of groceries to bring in and again, the house was dark. Plus, she was tired, of course. She was always tired. She thought of calling Suzie's cell phone to ask her to come help with the groceries, but the odds of that happening were slim to none. For one thing, for a techie kid, Suzie rarely had her cell phone on. Amanda's message would then go to voice mail, which was a waste of money because Suzie never listened to her messages. Or, if she did, she wouldn't bother to respond. Even if the phone was charged up and turned on, Suzie would be unable to hear it with her headphones on. Why in the world that kid insisted on wearing headphones when she was the only person in the house was beyond her. She just seemed to like them. The one time Amanda tried them, the constant pressure gave her a headache, plus the set was so efficient at cancelling out noise, that Amanda had felt like she was buried underwater.

Glancing three doors down, she spied Ben and his son Kyle on their front lawn. With glass jars, they were trying to capture fire flies. She could hear Kyle's squeals and giggles as his dad lunged and tackled him to the ground, ending with tickles. At least the weather wasn't getting them down.

She pushed open the driver's door and put one foot onto her driveway. Something squished. Oh, god, let that be mud. Mud, on her paved drive? Watching where she placed her other foot, Amanda got out and inspected her shoe, her treasured Manola Blahnik bought on eBay. Damn that neighbor's Rottweiler. She moved to the grass and began to gingerly scrape her foot, careful not to scratch the leather. But, the cut-outs in the side of shoe let her down. They were part of what had attracted her to the pair in the first place, but the decorative holes in the sides let the questionable substance ooze in onto her foot, her hose offering little protection. Not only was her foot assaulted by the dog's offering, but also her nose. What did they feed that brute? And why did they let him get rid of it on her property.

Amanda gingerly toed off the offending shoe, accidently smearing dog droppings onto the toe of her other shoe. She searched her pockets for a tissue but came up with only a wrapped mint of questionable age. She padded in her stocking feet through the puddles to the trunk. She emptied one of her grocery bags, scattering the contents throughout the darkened trunk. The empty sack provided a combination of glove and bag to pick up her ruined shoes and carry them into the house. She tied the bag tightly closed, promising herself she'd deal with her footwear later. They could be recovered, she was sure of it. It had to be possible.

Her hose were ruined already, so Amanda waded through another puddle, trying to scrape off the worst of the stink and stickiness. Then, walking to the back of the house, she found the garden hose that was looped up for the winter. The tap brought frigid water bursting out, soaking her skirt before she was able to direct the stream onto her feet. She blasted them until they were numb, turning the sides and soles over and over until only pale skin showed. Next, she washed any bits the grass that had soaked farther into the lawn where hopefully she would not walk. Or Suzie wouldn't walk. Imagine what a fit Suzie would pitch if this had happened to her. Amanda half-smiled at the thought, then scolded herself. What kind of a mother would laugh at her child's misfortune when she knew how upset Suzie would be? Still....

"Suzie," Amanda called. "Get up here, I need some help." Amanda perched on the doorsill, afraid to step into the kitchen in case she made a mess. It was too dark outside to see just how well she'd cleaned her feet.

No footsteps coming up from the basement.

Amanda stamped on the floor. She picked up a boot from the shoe rack and banged on the door. Nothing. She yelled.

"Mom, I'm in the middle of something. Can't you get it yourself?"

"No, damn it, Suzie, I can't. Get up here right now!"

When there was no immediate response, Amanda yelled, "Suzie!" and threw the boot against the basement door, startling herself. Where had that come from? She was not a throwing kind of person, could never remember throwing something in anger in her life. What was the matter with her? But in some quirky way, it had felt kind of good.

Suzie emerged from the basement, grumpy, disheveled. "What do you want?" she demanded.

"Look at me."

Suzie raised her eyes to her mother. "What are you doing in bare feet?

Your panty hose are tattered. And, where are your shoes?"

Amanda rattled the plastic bag.

"Wilson's Rottweiler left another deposit on our property, this time right beside where I get out of my car. I stepped right in it. I think my good shoes are ruined."

Suzie's nose wrinkled and she took a step back. She placed one finger under her nose.

"I need you to go to my room and bring me a pair of socks - big slouch socks that are easy to put on and go to the bathroom and bring me a towel."

Suzie stood looking at her in disgust.

"Now!" barked Amanda.

Suzie turned and hustled away. Well, thought Amanda. Maybe I should speak to her like that more often. Suzie rarely obeyed that easily, especially when it was something she didn't want to do.

Amanda slid her butt down the wall until she was sitting on the floor. She took the towel from Suzie's outstretched fingertips, one hand still blocking off her nostrils. Carefully, gingerly, she wiped off her feet, then slowly eased on the socks. There. Now she could at least make it to the shower without turning her house into a haz-mat site. She tossed the towel into the bag with her shoes; she'd deal with that later as well.

Walking down the hall to the bathroom, she told Suzie to go bring in the groceries from the car and take an extra sack with her to collect the food that was loose in the trunk.

Suzie blanched. "But what if I walk in the dog poo, too? It stinks. I can't go near that. You know that I hate smells."

"Yeah, well, so do I. I have to get myself cleaned up and you have to bring in our groceries."

Suzie just stared at her.

Amanda sighed. "Walk around the other side of the car if you have to. This stuff was by the driver's door. Go out the front door, and take a wide circle on the grass to the back of the car. Or walk around the passenger side. I don't care how, just do it!"

"But it's dark out there."

"I noticed. It's dark every night when I get home. That's why I asked you to have the outside lights on for me. Remember?"

Nervously looking through the curtain, Suzie admitted that she forgot.

"Figure it out, kid." Amanda left to shower off the muck and the experience.

Sitting on the side of the tub, Amanda swiveled her feet inside, stripped off the socks and stuck her feet under the faucet, the water as hot as she could stand it. She poured liquid soap on her soles, over and over before daring to use her hands to scrub. Only when there were absolutely no signs of brown on her or in the tub did she stand and adjust the shower.

The cascade of wet warmth poured over Amanda, washing away not only Rover's leavings, but some of the cares of the day. While her responsibilities weren't over for the day, at least she could take this time to herself, time to relax and unwind and maybe pamper herself just a bit. Suzie was doing the heavy lifting for the moment. Wouldn't it be sweet to exit this shower to the smells of supper cooking? But no, that was not likely to happen. Still, just having the groceries inside and put away was a nice start.

She thought back over her conversation with Suzie. Conversation. Was yelling at your kid considered a conversation? Whatever, she got some action out of her and some help. And, maybe Suzie had gotten the point about how unwelcoming it was to come home to a dark house.

The waning hot water reminded her that she could not stay in the shower all evening. There was still work to be done. Amanda got out, but took her time. Her morning showers were always rushed; not being a morning person, she never seemed to leave herself enough time so that she didn't have to hurry. This evening shower business was nice. She'd taken the time to shave her legs. Wrapping her hair in a towel, she slathered lotion all over. Swathed in a bath sheet, she crossed into her bedroom for the fluffy, fleece robe that hung on the back of her door. Tattered, but comfy.

Should she go start supper now? Naw, what would a few more minutes matter?

She rummaged under the bathroom sink for the facial mask she'd bought on impulse months ago. Now seemed a good time to try it out. Reading the directions, she smeared the stuff on, grinning at her ghostly face in the mirror. Twenty minutes until it came off. She could feel her skin tightening under the goo. Unwinding the towel, she shook out her hair and ran a comb through the tangles. A ragged fingernail edge snagged a strand. Lowering the toilet seat, Amanda sat down and went to work with the nail file. Then she moved on to her toes, clipping and shaping, then painting those nails. Should her fingernails match or could they be a color all their own? This time of year no one saw her toes but herself, she who cared?

As she waited for the polish to set, she took out her blow dryer. Doing something just a bit different, she styled her hair. Not bad. She looked at her watch. Another seven minutes before the mask should come off, enough time to begin dinner.

Padding to the kitchen, Amanda appreciated its pristine state. Suzie had done a good job. The only thing out of order was the plastic bag she'd dropped by the door. She'd see to those shoes after supper; they weren't going anywhere. Looking around, she noticed that the outside lights were back off. Well, Suzie must have turned them off after coming back in. No matter. They were tucked in for the night now. She checked the locks, but found the one to the kitchen door still unlocked. Well, no harm if Suzie forgets that one little thing. It was fixed now.

Planning to cook up a batch of savory crepes, Amanda turned to the fridge. Maybe a glass of chardonnay while she cooked. Hmm. None in the fridge and she'd just bought a bottle when she got the groceries. Suzie must have put it in the cupboard. Not drinking wine herself, she might not have realized it should be kept cold. Rummaging for the eggs, Amanda came up short. She knew they'd been out; that's why she picked up a dozen after work. Suzie definitely knew that eggs belonged in the fridge. Something pricked at the back of Amanda's cerebral cortex.

She checked the fruit bowl on the counter. No bananas. She checked the cereal cupboard for the box of corn flakes she'd just bought. Not there. Peering out the kitchen window, she looked towards her car. A faint glow showed from the still open trunk.

"Suzie!"

CHAPTER 5

Again, "Suzie!" Nothing. Opening the basement door, Amanda made out the faint tinny sound of loud music coming through the wrong side of headphones. She marched down the stairs.

Hands on hips, she regarded her daughter. Suzie's eyes were glued to her computer monitor, her head bobbing faintly to the beat of some song, oblivious to Amanda's presence. She strode to the computer and stood close.

Suzie raised her eyes to see her mom. Her head jerked back and she stood, causing the castor chair to overturn. Suzie's wide eyes stared at her mother and she backed up another couple steps.

"What's the matter with you? Where are those groceries? And why are you staring at me like that? Suzie, explain what's going on. I left you to do a simple job and it's not done."

Suzie just stared.

Amanda scowled hard and felt her face crack. She brought her hand to her forehead. Oh, yeah. The face mask.

"I was giving myself a facial and forgot that it's time to take it off now." She turned toward the stairs. "I have to go take care of this. While I do that, you go bring those groceries in and put them away."

She was part way up the stairs when a little voice said, "I can't."

Turning back, Amanda asked, "Can't? Why?"

Suzie's hands moved out to the sides and her fingers flicked. "It's dark out there, mom. And, there's stuff I might step in, stuff that stinks and might squish."

Normally Amanda was moved by her daughter's hand flapping and would back down. Anything to prevent that stress from building up in

Suzie's body. But not this time. Perhaps she wouldn't win mother of the year award, but she'd had it.

Rounding on Suzie, Amanda's voice rose. "Do you think I like the smell of that stuff? Do you think I like stepping in dog shit? Do you think I like going to work each and every day then coming home to a dark house? Stumbling through the darkness to bring in the groceries, and then cooking supper for you, begging you to come and eat with me? Do you think I like that? Any of that?"

Suzie could have been a wax statue. Stiff, yet ready to melt in the sun, or the heat of her mother's words. Amanda didn't yell, at least hardly ever. Suzie didn't know when she'd seen her mother let loose like this. "No," her soft whisper said.

"No! What do you mean no? I asked you to do a few simple things and you tell me 'no'?"

"No, I mean I was answering your question. Your questions. You asked a whole bunch in a row without giving me time to think about any of them or give you a response. I think the answer to all of them was no, but I may have forgotten some. You spoke awfully fast."

"What the hell are you talking about?"

"Your questions. You asked me things like if I think you like the smell, do you like stepping in it, do you like going to work each day and coming home in the dark and begging me and I think I missed some of them there. But as much as I can remember, the answer was no,"

"Suzie, those were rhetorical questions. Remember we talked about that. Rhetorical questions are ones people ask but they don't expect an answer."

"Why would you ask the questions then?"

"Because, well, just because. That's the way people talk sometimes." Amanda shook her head. "That's beside the point." At Suzie's puzzled look, she explained, "It doesn't matter. What matters is that there is work to be done and I could use a little help around here. Now get up here." She turned and climbed the stairs.

After a few seconds, Suzie's lighter, quieter footsteps followed. Suzie huddled near the open basement door, barely into the kitchen. She studied the floor.

Hardening herself to her daughter's frail appearance and timid expression, Amanda broke it down. "First, go turn on the outside lights."

Suzie's head turned in both directions. "Where are they?"

She didn't know which switches turned on the outside lights? She'd only lived here her entire life.

"Go to the front door and try the switches there. Watch out the window to see when you've got the outside ones on. Then, go to the back door and do the same thing." Suzie hesitated but Amanda's look said it all. She just waited. When that was done, she continued.

"Get an extra grocery bag out of the pantry." Again, Suzie didn't seem to know where to go. Amanda strode to the cupboard, held open the door and pointed. Suzie bent to sort through the jumble of mashed bags and came up with one in each hand.

"Go put on your shoes and a jacket."

"What do you want me to do with the bags?"

"Suzie..."

Returning with an unzipped jacket and runners, Suzie's shoulders slumped. "You're not going to make me go outside, are you?"

"That's exactly where you're going. Those groceries need to come in. That trunk's been open for over an hour now with the light on and its drizzling out."

"That means some of the stuff might be soggy by now."

"Exactly."

"Well, I can't touch anything like that."

"Tell me, Suzie, how is that the boxes might have gotten soggy?"

"It's raining out."

"And who was supposed to bring the groceries in?"

"You asked me to but I couldn't; I can't. You know how I hate smells - they make me feel all funny and my brain freezes up. And I don't like being out alone in the dark. You know that."

"Take a look. You've turned on the lights so it's no longer dark. You can see well enough to get in. And you won't step in any hidden offerings because you can see where you're going with the lights on."

"Can't you help me?" Was that a whine in the voice of a twenty-one year old? Oh, it was high time Amanda set some rules around here.

"No. I can't. I have to get supper going. Maybe you should be thinking of ways that you can help me."

"I am. I'm bringing in your damn groceries." The door slammed behind Suzie.

A quiet Suzie sat across the kitchen table from her mother without being asked or nagged. She picked at her food, a meal she usually enjoyed - savory crepes with shrimp and mushrooms and scallions.

"Want to talk about it?"

"No," Suzie replied.

"I wasn't exactly asking if you did."

"But that is what you said. Mom, can't you just say what you mean? It's tiring trying to figure out what your words mean."

"We need to talk about what happened before supper." Suzie didn't look up, so Amanda continued. She'd been thinking about how to approach this. She'd hollered earlier and that had worked but was not ideal. She'd try gentle this time.

"You did something hard tonight."

Suzie looked up, surprised. Did she receive compliments from her mother so seldom or did she expect to be yelled at again?

"I know it was hard for you to go out to bring in the groceries, but you did it anyway. That's the definition of brave, in my books." She waited a minute. "How hard was it?" she asked.

"Not as hard as I thought it might be. It was at first - I just hated going out the door. From inside here looking out, it seemed so dark and the car looked a long ways away. But once I got out there, it wasn't so far. Twenty-six steps exactly. Twenty-six there, then a few extra while I fished around for the groceries, then twenty-six back to the kitchen door. It might have been less if I'd used the front door, but that is not the way we usually enter, so I didn't try it."

"You could have, you know. I didn't care which door you used, just that the groceries made it in here."

Suzie shook her head. "That's not how we do it."

"Sometimes there can be more than one way to do something. But, it's okay to go with what you're comfortable with as long as it works. We need to work on you being more flexible, though." She helped herself to another crepe. "Roughly how long did that chore take you?"

"I know exactly. Six minutes, forty-three seconds. I noticed the time on the stove when I left and came back. I would have done it in less time if someone hadn't dumped groceries all over the trunk. It took as much time to dig them out and load them in a bag as it did to walk them back here."

"So, seven minutes if we count putting on your coat and shoes. That's not much time out of your day. How long did it take you to put the groceries away?"

"I didn't watch the time for that. I wasn't worried about being out in the dark or coming across poop in the kitchen, so I just put things away. You know, you didn't organize this kitchen very well. Some of the places you keep things are not logical. It took me longer because I was trying to adapt to your system when it really doesn't make sense."

"So, fix it."

"What?"

"Fix it. Tomorrow, your job is to re-organize this kitchen, making it orderly and more efficient."

Suzie's face showed some interest. "Really? You mean I can put stuff wherever I think it should be?"

"Yep. I know it's not right. Over time stuff just got thrown in places. It'd be a real help if you organized this space for us."

She received a half-smile for this.

"Now here's the rest of what I wanted to talk about. In total, the chores you did today took about fifteen minutes or so - that includes bringing in the groceries and putting them away. Now, think about the chores that I did. I spent about half an hour making supper for us. So far, I've spent twice as much time as you doing household chores today. Now that we're finished eating, the dishes need to be put in the dishwasher and the kitchen cleaned up. Who do you think should do that?"

"Moooom, I have stuff I need to get back to. I was in the middle of a game when you yelled for me. Some of these online gamers get nasty if you leave them hanging for too long. I could get kicked out. And you always do the kitchen stuff."

"Right, I do. That changes right now. Here's the thing. There are two adults living in this house with only one of them doing pretty much all the work. That might have been all right when you were a child, but you're not a kid any longer. You're a young woman. Maybe it's my fault that I didn't expect you to act like one, but that is going to change. Two adults sharing a house share responsibilities as well."

"Geez, Mom, we're doing all right. We get along pretty good. You only yell sometimes and we try not to get on each other's nerves. I'm quiet at night like you want me to be."

"That's true, but it's not good enough, not any longer. We'll start small, with a chore list."

"I hate chores."

"Me, too."

"Yeah, but you do them all the time."

"That's part of being an adult, doing things because they have to be done, whether or not you feel like it."

"I don't see why we need to change anything." She looked around the house. "The place looks all right to me and we've been doing it this way for years."

"My fault. I forgot how grown up you are. I'm not doing you any favors by sheltering you from responsibilities. Todd has been telling me that for years but it's only just penetrating my tired old brain."

"Oh, so this is all Uncle Todd's fault. Why doesn't he mind his own business?"

"He thinks we are his business. He's family. And, he's right."

Suzie got up from the table and headed for the basement.

"Ahem," Amanda reminded. When Suzie stopped and turned, Amanda pushed back from the table and nodded toward the dirty dishes. "Remember? I've already put in over twice as much time as you on chores tonight." She pointed at the table, counter and stove. "Your turn."

Did Suzie actually flounce? Amanda thought so, but at least she came back to the table and began stacking the dishes. Amanda wondered how many might make it to the dishwasher intact.

As she walked toward the living room, Amanda called, "Who is making up the chore list, you or me?"

"Neither! I'm not doing it. I'm too busy to take on your work."

CHAPTER 6

"You know, if your dad was here, he'd be proud of you. He liked to tackle things that were hard for him. Many of his challenges were in sports and competitions, like his softball league. He says he never was a great hitter, but he liked to try anyway. He kept that signed Louisville Slugger bat as a reminder of what can happen when someone gives it their all. Remember that bat? You used to try to swing it when you were little."

"If dad was here, you wouldn't be trying to get me to do your chores. You'd be ragging on him to do them and I'd be left alone."

Amanda let that one go.

"Besides, he didn't exactly do the hard stuff did he? He left when he found out that I had Asperger's Syndrome, that I was not the perfect, normal child he wanted."

How to explain. Was there any way to explain away that kind of hurt? Likely not. "You're right. He didn't stick around when things got hard." She thought about it. "Your father was good at challenging himself physically and team competitions were really important to him. He always had to be in a group, the center of attention and the action. That's part of what attracted me to him, his energy and his confidence."

"I'm not sure his leaving had much to do with you. I think he was tiring of me. After a few years of being together, things weren't exciting enough for him. He craved excitement and competition. I didn't compete with him. I settled into the pattern of married life and caring for our beautiful little girl.

"Suzie, there were so many perfect things about you. I could hold a conversation with you when most kids your age were still stuck on single words. Your language skills blew other mothers out of the water when we went to the park."

"I told them to get out of the pool?"

Amanda grinned and squeezed Suzie's hand. "That's a figure of speech. They were very surprised that a child as young as you could speak so well."

"Why didn't my dad like that?"

"Oh, he did. He was proud of you. But the things that were important to him didn't matter to you, or to me. When you were three, he enrolled you in T-ball. It was a disaster. You had no interest in the game or really in playing with the other kids. You had interests of your own. Then your dad tried you in ballet and in figure skating, then soccer, none of which interested you. Lots of little kids that age would not have liked those sports either. Maybe if he'd waited a few years it would have been different. But you didn't want to be there; you didn't understand the demands the instructors were putting on you or why you had to do things in a group and in certain ways. You got overwhelmed and upset. Your father didn't know how to handle it. The more he pushed, the more upset you became until it carried over into school."

"I was five when I got the diagnosis, wasn't I?"

"Yes. Dwayne wasn't much of a reader. While we were waiting for the appointment, I read everything I could find on autism and Asperger's Syndrome. Much of what I read seemed to fit you. Because I read so much, I got a better handle on it than your dad. I knew that it was just a label to describe some of the characteristics you had. It wasn't anything bad or wrong, just different. And the more I read, the more I could see how other people helped their kids and all the things that children with Asperger's could do."

"Yeah, I might have been able to do stuff, but it wasn't enough for him. He still left."

There was not a way to soften this. "Yes, he did. That says more about him than it does about you. He missed out and it's his loss."

"It doesn't feel that way to me."

Amanda put an arm around Suzie's shoulder and squeezed her hard. Suzie tolerated it for a few seconds, and then pulled away with a, "Mooom."

"I never wanted to speak ill of your father. I wanted you to have positive memories of him. But maybe I should tell you some things now that you're an adult.

"Your dad loved to have a good time. He craved excitement and parties. Normal family life bored him. He could only spend so much quiet time at home with me without being restless and edgy and needing to be around a crowd. That's why his sports meant so much to him. I'm not sure Dwayne knew how to live well within his own skin. Too much time to sit and reflect seemed to make him antsy. In some ways he was like a kid himself and not ready to accept the responsibility of being a parent. Caring for someone else interfered with his fun. That's my fault; I should have recognized that in him earlier. But I thought I could make up for his lack; he'd provide the excitement in your life and I'd be the day-to-day stable one."

"You did, Mom. You were always there."

Amanda regarded her daughter. "You know, I think I did not too bad a job when you were younger, but these last years, I've fell down at my job. Uncle Todd helped me see that."

"Oh, that's just Uncle Todd. We're fine the way we are. Sure, we are. We don't need to change anything."

"Yes, we do sweetie. I'm tired. I'm tired of doing it all. It's not fair to me and it's not fair to you, either. This is not how life is and I'm not helping you prepare yourself."

"Ah, Mom...."

"Here's the deal. We're drawing up that chore list. Tomorrow on my lunch hour, I'll type out a list of all the chores that need to be done around here in a week. Then we'll put them in two columns - yours and mine. We'll divide things up evenly."

"NO! I won't do it. Uncle Todd can come over here and do chores if he's so bothered about it. I like things the way they are." Suzie stood and began pacing. Her voice rose with each back and forth stride. She waved her hands. The tears came. She ranted about all the things she had to do, all the time these stupid chores would take, how her mother was destroying her life, how Todd was ruining everything. The sobbing started so that it was difficult for Amanda to make out the words. Just as well. Amanda was steeling herself not to cave in. Every time before, Amanda had given in to Suzie's tantrums; anything to keep the peace. And yes, these were tantrums. When Amanda tried to sit back and watch her daughter objectively, these were not too different than the toddler tantrums they'd lived through when Suzie was small.

Change was hard; how often had she heard that? For Suzie, change seemed especially hard. Amanda had believed that this was due to the Asperger's Syndrome influence. Everyone with Asperger's had trouble with flexibility and change.

Now, as she regarded her daughter on the floor, she wondered. Suzie had upped her game. From a vertical, screaming, crying, tantrumming twenty-one year old, she had become a horizontal, screaming, crying, tantrumming twenty-one year old. Had she actually thrown herself onto the floor? Yep. Her fists and feet beat on the carpet, but Amanda noted that unlike her childhood counterpart, Suzie no longer banged her head. Nothing she did was actually hurting herself; there would be no bruises.

Amanda rose to make herself a cup of tea. Where were those tea bags?

Suzie had actually re-organized the room, but now Amanda couldn't find anything. Ah, there they were.

Was the noise from Suzie's storm lessening or was it just that Amanda was farther away from the eye of the tornado? No, it seemed quieter. She tiptoed back down the hallway and peeked into the living room. Suzie was still on the floor and her hands still beat an irregular tattoo on the floor, but she'd angled her body around until she could peer into the hallway where her mother had disappeared. Their eyes locked.

Immediately, the volume of Suzie's shrieks rose several notches and her heels resumed their pounding. Hmmm.

Amanda backed away. Well, that told her a lot.

What to do next? Should she take her tea into her bedroom? Her rocking chair with a good book sounded relaxing. Or, maybe her book, the tea and a bubble bath would make better companions. Anything was better than being with Suzie at the moment.

No, here she was being critical of Suzie's aversion to change, when really she herself was attempting to duck change just as badly. Escaping to her room or a soothing tub was the chicken way out. She'd started down this path, so she should follow through. To back down now would make it all that much harder to attempt this again.

Really, was she helping Suzie by avoiding these issues? Todd was right, much as Amanda hated to admit it. Darn, she'd always hated it when he was right. Watching Suzie pitch her two year old-type fit, had opened Amanda's eyes. Her daughter was truly throwing a tantrum, and not even a twenty-one year old fit, just a variation on what she'd done as a child. Or, Amanda admitted, throughout her teen years. These storms had come less often these last few years, but was it because Suzie had herself under better control, or was it that Amanda tiptoed around, careful to never raise contentious issues. Or put demands on her daughter.

Lifting her chin, Amanda entered the living room. When Suzie spied her, the shrieks rose in volume, but there was a new twist. Suzie had moved herself off the floor and now lay prostrate on the couch. The couch where Amanda usually sat to watch television.

"Excuse me," Amanda said as she placed her tea on the coffee table. "I'd like to sit down now."

Suzie wailed away, but didn't budge.

Amanda perched herself on the edge of the couch, near Suzie's legs and pushed herself in. It was a calculated risk, but she thought Suzie's aversion to touch would be stronger than the possibility that she'd kick out at her mother.

She was right. Sort of. As she edged herself deeper into the couch, Suzie recoiled in surprise, pulling her legs up to her chest. As Amanda settled back, Suzie bellowed, "No, no, no! Get off! This is my spot. I'm upset; I can't stand it!" When Amanda didn't budge, Suzie pulled her knees tighter into her chest, then uncoiled, her momentum throwing her feet against her mom's hip and thigh. Amanda had been about to take a sip of her chamomile tea. The kick caused her wrist to turn, spilling some of the scalding liquid onto Amanda's lap, but most landed on Suzie's feet and ankles.

Her shrieks split the air. "Ow, I'm burnt, I'm scalded! It hurts, it hurts, it hurts!" She drew her feet back protectively to her chest. "Look what you did," she accused. "You burned me." The wails turned to sobs.

Amanda's thigh hurt and she pulled the sodden fabric away from her skin. Good thing she was wearing her baggy jeans. Yes, it hurt, but more in the uncomfortable range, certainly the tea was not hot enough to warrant the fuss Suzie was making.

She brought the tea to her lips and sipped. Yes, it was definitely hot, too hot to gulp, but not in the dangerous range. She regarded her daughter over the rim, glad that she had not filled the cup to the brim. Did Suzie have any idea what she looked like? How she sounded? How much had she, as her mother, contributed to this behavior? Had she let things get so out of control that an intelligent girl like Suzie could actually think that this was normal behavior?

"You don't care," sobbed Suzie. "My mother doesn't care that I've been injured." Her crying continued, but was toned down a few notches.

Amanda reached over and snagged the remote off the table. She turned on the television and began channel surfing. As soon as she settled on a channel, her daughter's wails rose again, drowning out the voices on the television.

The old Amanda might have entered into a nagging match with Suzie, telling her to be quiet, admonishing her for her lack of consideration, yada, yada, yada. But that kind of response might have led to this point.

Instead, Amanda had an idea. She was not a techie person, but maybe this would work. Years ago, when Suzie suffered badly from noise sensitivity, Amanda used a set of wireless headphones to watch television when Suzie was trying to sleep. Maybe they'd still work. The transmitter peeked out from behind debris collected on the television stand, dusty and unused. She rummaged in the magazine rack where she used to keep the headphones. Yep, there they were under ancient flyers and old magazines and two photo albums. She really did need to sort through this junk. Ignoring Suzie, she put them on and blessedly, the canned laughter from the sitcom flowed into her ears. And bonus, they muted out the racket her kid was making. Keeping her face as bland as possible, Amanda sipped her tea and watched TV.

Suzie stomped the couch with her bent knees, but didn't attempt to kick her mother again. But, she made the ride as uncomfortable as possible for Amanda. Amanda marveled at her daughter's stamina; it must be good exercise for the abs to continue bouncing like that, not that a kid as thin as Suzie needed to worry about flabby abs. Suzie's sobbing quieted, with the just occasional hiccup and whining ahhh sound, although she barely remained still for more than a minute.

When the show was over, Amanda thought she'd stayed long enough to make her point. She stretched and yawned and moved toward the edge of the couch. "Well, I think I'm off to bed now. Good night."

Amanda smiled to herself as she undressed. Was it mean to laugh at your daughter? But the look on Suzie's face was comical when Amanda left the room.

Then the fairer side of Amanda second guessed herself. What kind of a mother would play mind games with her child? Suzie was in acute stress; that much was apparent. Why else would an adult choose to act in that fashion? She was firmly entrenched in a pattern and strenuously objected to her mom's plans to change things.

But, Suzie really did have problems. She was not like other twenty-one year olds. To be honest, she was not like fifteen year olds, really. Her inability to manage her emotions was a serious weakness. How would she ever be able to handle a job if she reacted that way to frustrations? To demands put on her? She'd never survive in Amanda's workplace or be able to handle the stuff that got thrown her way on a daily basis. Good thing Suzie had a strong mother.

But, what if she didn't? What if something happened to her? That struck-by-a-bus thing really did happen to people. How in the world would Suzie manage without her mother? She could barely manage when Amanda did everything for her. Maybe Todd was right and things had to change. But how?

☐

CHAPTER 7

"Hey, Mandy," Todd said into the phone. "Is Suzie ready to be dragged through the dirt in our Scrabble match Saturday?"

"Saturday?"

"Yeah. Remember I said I'd come over Saturday and hang with Suzie so that you and what's his name could go out? You know, that guy who called you the night I was there, the one you were so cagey about."

"Oh, I told him no. I'm not really into dating."

Silence. Accusing silence. Her brother never felt compelled to keep his opinions to himself, no matter how many strong nonverbal cues Amanda gave him. "Why?" he asked. He was obviously restraining himself.

"You know that my situation is not normal. I'm not free to pursue a relationship the way other women are. My first duty has to be to my child and as you are well aware, she needs me."

Silence.

To fill the void, Amanda continued. "Maybe this won't last forever; Maybe Suzie will get it together all of a sudden and feel brave, want to do things, want to be with other people." Then I can have more of a life, she added to herself.

"Why?"

"Have you any idea how frustrating you are when you speak in one word sentences?"

"I mean, why would Suzie want to change anything? Look, you know I think she's a great kid and I love her like she was my own, but honestly, why on earth would she want to change? Think about what she likes. Computers and music. She's got both - a better computing system than most people could dream up. She has access to anything that takes her fancy in the technology realm. You buy it for her. She mentions it and magically it appears."

"It's not like I'm spoiling her. This is the only thing she has going in her life. She leads such a bare existence compared to other kids her age; computer stuff is all she has. And, it's not that expensive. What if she had a thing about designer clothes or wanted a sports car? I'd be spending a lot more of those things than I do on her tech gadgets."

"True." Todd was placating her. She could tell by his voice, so she braced herself for what was coming next. "But, how would those other twenty-one year olds acquire their fancy clothes or wheels? Most would be earning the money for these things themselves through a job."

"Suzie has a job. She's working on developing her graphics skills so she can take on online contract jobs. And, she's creating music she'll sell over the internet. And, she's creating anime cartoons that she'll turn into a book."

"Mandy, listen to yourself. Do you honestly believe that? A job is something that generates an income. Even a volunteer job at least gives something to other people."

"Yes, damn it, I do believe it. I believe in Suzie. My daughter is talented. She's capable of so much. And, when she's ready, she'll be able to give to other people."

"At least we can agree on that part of it. Yep, she has potential. But her piddling around on the computer for the last three years has brought in, now let's see, how much income was that?"

"You jerk, you know that she's not earned any money from those things yet. But she will. She talks about her growing skills with this rendering program."

"Hmm. How much call is there for a skilled renderer in your basement?"

"She'll connect with people online. She told me how she saw requests on a site called Fivver for things she thinks she could do."

"Fivver. Yes, I've heard of it. Do you know where it got its name?" When Amanda didn't answer, he continued. "Because the jobs there paid five dollars. It's expanded since then, but lots of job bids are for low numbers like that. This is not something Suzie could do to support herself or even to contribute to her upkeep."

"Well, she's learning still; it takes time, you know, to develop these computer skills."

"Right, it does. That's why there are post-secondary courses devoted to just that, teaching students these skills so that they can then go out and earn a living."

"We're not going there. High school was such an awful experience for her; it was all I could do to keep her going until graduation. She is not trying school again. Even if she could survive it, I couldn't."

Silence. Then, "Amanda, it's not about you."

Amanda's voice got louder. "Don't you think I know that? Everything's about Suzie, my life is all about Suzie. That's all I think about. Who do you think has supported her all these years? Where would she have been without me?"

"I repeat, it's not about you. Yes, you've definitely been her rock and you've done all the parenting and heavy lifting since Dwayne left - maybe even before then. I worry that you're seeing your role now as Suzie's support."

"Well, I am. Who else does she have?"

"She has me, a little, but I don't think Suzie's support system should be the focus. We should be working on Suzie supporting Suzie."

"Don't you think I don't know that? What I wouldn't give for her to be able to be like other kids her age. But every time I try to put pressure on her, she melts down. You've seen it, but not at its worst. She shakes. She gets red, her whole body vibrates. She sobs for hours. The anxiety attacks are awful and then she's a wreck for days, not able to do anything, not even the computer stuff she loves.

More quietly, Amanda continued. "Things are such a struggle for her. Suzie needs time. She's just not there yet."

"When, Amanda, when will she be ready? And how will you know it?'

Half an hour later, the phone rang again.

"Me, again," said Todd. "I thought I'd give you time to cool off in case you weren't speaking to me."

"Todd, yes you tick me off sometimes, but I am still speaking to you. I know you mean well, but you're not here; you don't live with Suzie and see just how much things affect her."

"I know, sis. It's bad. Sometimes when you're stuck in a rut though, it's hard to see the pattern. I think you need a plan, we need a plan. Just treading this same path is not working for either of you."

"If you're going to talk pills again, I'm hanging up."

"Yeah, medication is one thing that might be able to help."

"I'm not having Suzie changed into a zombie or a drug addict. You think we have enough to deal with now, wait until she's addicted."

"Mandy, that wouldn't happen. You wouldn't let it. And no one, especially a doctor, would want to turn a good kid into an addict. But that's not what meds do. Nor, does anyone want her to be a zombie. If someone on meds seems overly sedated, then that's the wrong medication or the wrong dose. Those things would not happen to Suzie because you'd be monitoring how she's affected by the pills and reporting to her doctor. Plus, Suzie can tell you how she feels. Between you, Suzie and the doctor, you'd

Autism Grows Up

get it right. What could a trial hurt?"

"None of that will be happening because Suzie is fine the way she is. I'll not have her doped up or changed."

"Fine? Do you really think she's fine right now? Come on, Mand, life's passing her by and she's not getting better. Something has to give."

"Likely you're the one who's going to give, because I'm not budging on this issue."

"Maybe you're not budging, but what does Suzie have to say about it? She's an adult and adults are in charge of their own body."

"Suzie may be an adult in number of years, but mentally, she is not. She's really a child in need of her mother's protection and care."

"If that's what you truly believe, then let's make it legal."

"What do you mean?"

"You can have Suzanne declared legally incompetent and in need of a guardian. You, you'd be her guardian, in charge of her financial affairs, medical and living arrangements. And the agreement would state that if anything happened to you, guardianship would fall to me, or whomever you want."

Amanda stood and paced with the phone to her ear. Her voice rose. "My daughter is an intelligent young woman, incredibly intelligent. She has all sorts of potential. You're making her sound incompetent."

Todd waited. And waited. "Mandy, this is what's known as a pregnant pause. Pretend I'm a stranger. Humor me and describe a day in Suzie's life to me."

Sigh. "She gets up, well, I'm not sure when she gets up. On the weekends when I'm not at work, I'd say she appears around early to mid-afternoon. She tends to get set in her routines so I'd guess that it's about the same during the work week. She heads downstairs right away and turns on her computer. She's down there a while, so maybe she checks her email or I don't know what. After a bit she wanders back upstairs and pours a cup of coffee - with skim milk and four sugars." Amanda shuddered. The stuff was like syrup. "Usually I offer to make her some lunch then, but I think when she's here alone she throws some leftovers in the microwave. At least from the dirty dishes stashed around her desk, it looks like she's heating up food that we had for supper the night before. I always make sure I've made enough for her lunch the next day."

"She takes her food back to the computer and eats there. I don't know how long the actual eating part takes her, but likely hours. I worry about her causing food poisoning because the food sits so long and still, she scoops it into her mouth, a forkful every half hour or so. Or, at least it seems that way to me."

"What's she doing on the computer?"

"She spends a lot of time with the program called Blender

(http://www.blender.org/). It's an open-source software program they use for animation, making art, 3D stuff, video games and creating artwork. It's a pretty amazing program, I've been told, with huge capabilities. Suzie tried to explain it to me once - well, way more than once but I only grasp part of what she says. She tried to get me to watch this tutorial so I'd understand but it didn't really help me. (http://www.blender.org/support/tutorials/).

"So that's what she means when she talks about her art and drawing stuff?"

"Yes, that and rendering. I don't quite get it, but I think sometimes she draws stuff out of her own head and other times she calls it rendering. It's like she is trying to copy some object like a truck or tank from some game, brings it into Blender then creates her own spin on it with enhancements.

"She showed me this site she follows called, Fine Young Capitalists (https://www.indiegogo.com/projects/the-fine-young-capitalists--2) where they had this contest for young women developing video games."

"Did Suzie submit something?"

"Oh, no. She says she's not there yet, but she admires some of the work the contestants entered. She pledged some money and got a digital copy of the winning game, something about this ghost who builds a house in a town. She likes the character interactions as well as the building aspects. Oh, I remember now. It's called Afterlife Empire."

"So, she plays this game and does graphics modeling?"

"It's not just this game she plays. She likes something called, Halo, then there's the other sort of games she likes. I only remember the name of one, Gone Home. I remember that one because she said that even someone like me would like it, because I like reading and it has a great storyline. Or, so she says."

"You've told me that she games and makes art. Right?"

"She also follows some bloggers. There's this young man with autism named Travis Breeding and she follows his blog. (http://travisbreeding.com/). He also offers to help others with autism create blogs, and then turn their writing into books. Suzie is not a bad writer, you know."

"Is she working on a book? Did she start a blog with him?" Todd asked.

"She talks about it and says she's going to. I think she identifies with this guy and wants to be like him. Plus, Suzie is big into social issues. This one woman she tells me about, Susan Walsh, has a blog about disability issues (http://eastmeetswexx.blogspot.ca). Suzie cares about things other than autism. She's spent a lot of time reading and talking about his site called About Face that runs things like camps for kids who have facial differences. (http://www.aboutface.ca/)."

"Does Suzie want to volunteer there?"

Amanda shook her head. "She's never mentioned anything like that. I don't think she could, either. The camp is located here. So she could?" Amanda thought about it a minute more. "No, that would not be possible. She must know that because she's never mentioned it."

"Has she mentioned any other kind of volunteer work?"

"No, I think that would be too tough on her." A pause, then, "She listens to music; music seems to calm her."

"What kind of music?"

"Let me think. One singer she talks about is Sara Bareilles. She sings this song Suzie raves about; I listened and it's not bad. It's called, Brave. I think Suzie really identifies with it. The chorus is something about "I just want to see you be brave" or something like that. This Sara is almost like a hero to her. (https://www.youtube.com/watch?v=dyAfjUHlFSM)."

"Hm. So, she's inspired by someone telling her to be brave."

"Definitely."

"And what evidence do you see that she's taking this to heart and showing bravery?"

"Todd, you should see her when we have to leave the house for something. It takes her hours to prep, to brace herself for what she's going to face. Just greeting every day is an act of bravery for someone like Suzie."

"Mand, I'm trying not to harp on this, but what you've told me about Suzie's day sounds interesting."

Amanda interrupted. "She seems to find it fascinating. And, all-consuming."

"If this was someone else you were talking about, I'd think you were describing their hobbies. You know, those things we do when we have free time."

Amanda didn't reply.

Todd tried some more. "Most people consider their hobbies as their play time, those things adults do when those pesky responsibility things are done and out of the way."

"Your point is?"

"What are Suzie's responsibilities? Everyone has 'em. We all need them. Whether or not we like doing them, they are part of life, part of the stuff adults have to do. Where does Suzie fit with that?"

Amanda sighed into the phone. "She doesn't. She hates household responsibilities. She hates the feel and smell of dirty dishes or dirty laundry. She just wants to do her work, the stuff on the computer she likes."

"Don't we all," was muttered through the phone. Todd was not getting far with this. "Look Amanda, what I'm getting at is that everyone has some responsibilities; no one gets to just play all the time. But as far as I can see, that's all that Suzie does."

Amanda bristled. "She's learning all the time. And you should see some of the graphics she's created. She is really talented."

"That's great and I believe you about her talent. But how many people paint or knit or draw in their spare time? Those are hobbies.

"Living a life of self-indulgence is not helping Suzie and its sure not helping you either."

"Me? I'm fine. I'm getting by and looking after the two of us quite well, thanks."

"Yes, you're looking after the two of you. That's the point. It's all you and none of it is any effort on Suzie's part. You give and she takes. Life doesn't work like that; can't work like that. Everyone must contribute, at least in some way."

"Suzie will contribute - to this house and to the world someday. Someday when she's able. She won't be like this forever, you know."

"How do you know that? The longer someone sits in one pattern, the more stuck they get. And as far as I can see, Suzie is just about as entrenched as a person can be. Tell me, just how much improvement have you seen in the last year? The past two years?"

"Her graphics abilities have improved lots. You should see her renderings now compared to when she started with this program."

Todd stifled his impatience. "Mand, that's great and maybe one day that will turn into a useful skill for her. Right now it's an interest - an intense interest, even a passion, but it's a hobby."

"Amanda, I want more for my niece than that; she's capable of more. And, I don't get why you don't want more for her as well."

The phone slammed down in his ear.

☐

CHAPTER 8

The next evening was clear and warm. After making supper, and cleaning up the kitchen by herself, yet again, Amanda planted herself in the middle of the couch while Suzie retreated to her basement hideaway. Again.

The remote produced nothing watchable on television. Restless and trying not to give in to self-pity, Amanda headed out for a stroll around the neighborhood. She'd not go far or for too long, in case Suzie needed her.

Needed her. Hmph. Yeah, Suzie needed her to take care of all her basic needs. That was fine when Suzie was small, fine and expected. But would this never end? What would happen when Amanda grew too old to do it all? Would Suzie look after her then? The words 'fat chance' echoed in Amanda's mind.

"Evening, neighbor. It's a lovely evening for September?" It was Millie, an older woman who lived several doors down in a large house. Amanda's place might have been a carriage house for one of these larger places once upon a time.

Amanda stopped to chat from the sidewalk. Although Millie was older and past middle aged, she was pleasant company and they chatted from time to time. Middle aged? Actually, Amanda was now middle aged, she reminded herself. Millie must have at least twenty years on her. Amanda admired how alive Millie was and how she kept on after her husband's long illness and death several years ago.

"Come on up and sit a bit if you have time," invited Millie. "Grab a chair and I'll bring us some tea."

Amanda stretched out in a comfy Adirondack chair, a new addition, she noticed. There had been lots of improvements to the place since Millie had sold her house to Ben and Mel. They moved in with their son, Kyle, while

Millie remained, in the role of housekeeper. She got to keep living in the home she'd loved for most of her adult life but without the worry of upkeep and payments. She now had a nice cushion in case she needed it, plus a monthly salary for taking care of the family she loved. It might not work for some, but they all seemed happy. Happier than she and Suzie, at least.

"You're looking well, Millie," Amanda said as she cradled her mug of fragrant tea.

"Thanks, I am well. We're doing fine. But if you'll allow me to say so, I have seen you looking better. Are you all right my dear?"

"That obvious, eh?"

Millie nodded. "I don't mean to pry, but if you feel like talking, we have the porch to ourselves. The Wickens are out at the bakery." Ben's sister, Ellie ran the family bakery and Mel's brother worked there as chef. It was a family-friendly place and a favorite hang-out.

"They seem like a nice family. Mel's lucky to have a partner in raising her son. This single-parenting stuff is hard."

Millie looked over the rim of her cup. "Didn't you know? Mel's only been in Kyle's life for a couple years; she's his step-mother. Ben was a single dad for a while. Kyle only came to live with him when he turned five. That first year was rough for them both but Mel's been a blessing."

"I sympathize. But it's even harder when your kid has autism. Suzie actually has Asperger's Syndrome; it's a form of high functioning autism."

Millie nodded, without asking the usual stream of questions. "I've learned a lot about autism since Kyle came into our lives." When Amanda looked puzzled, she added, "You did know that Kyle has autism, didn't you?"

"No. I had no idea." Then she remembered. "Although, I did sort of wonder last summer. A couple times I heard him yelling; he was making a fuss about something with Mel in the backyard. She just stood and waited while he carried on. I admired her patience, but something about how Kyle was acting reminded me of Suzie when she was younger."

"Nice that even kids with autism grow out of things like tantrums, isn't it?"

Amanda studied her tea for a bit before mumbling, "Maybe not so much."

"Pardon me, dear?"

"I said, not so much. I mean Suzie is so much better in many ways. Her toddlerhood and preschool years were awful, but things got better as she matured." She waited, trying to decide how much to say, but Millie's kind eyes waited patiently and the words just started rolling out. "Millie, our lives are awful now. It was not so bad when Suzie was in school but since then, it's all fallen apart. I thought she'd be like other kids - finish school, get a job, maybe go to college, move out on her own, you know, become an adult.

"Instead, she's acting more like a self-indulgent child." There. She's said it. Amanda continued, "Honestly, Millie, Suzie is twenty-one years old. At her age, I'd been out on my own for a couple years, was married and expecting. I'd had a job at least part-time since I was sixteen. I looked after myself and my husband and our apartment. Suzie does none of that."

"Surely, she does some things. How does she spend her days?"

"On the computer. She has games she likes to play and she does some drawing, composes a bit, a very little bit, of music and fools around with some computer programming. She says she's learning and she likely is, but what for? My brother says these are all nice hobbies, but that Suzie is escaping from life."

"Is she looking for a job?"

Amanda shook her head. "In the beginning, there was talk of it, but the longer she was away from other people and the structure of having to go someplace every day like school, the more anxious she became until now she can hardly stand to leave the house, even with me."

"Does this bother her?"

"No. I don't think it bothers her at all. She seems, well, content. That is, until I start bugging her about something, about taking on some responsibility, on doing housework, that kind of thing. Then she is not content and hates that I'm bothering her."

"That anxiety thing bothers many people who have autism, at least that's what Mel tells me. She works a lot with Kyle on that so that his anxiety won't get out of control when he's older."

Amanda looked on with interest.

"She teaches him ways to relax himself when he starts to get too stressed. She's teaching him how to analyze situations because often his anxiety increases because he has misunderstood what's going on or he can't guess what will happen next. She writes these social stories and keeps a binder full of them that Kyle can refer to when he's getting stressed because of a new situation and he's unsure what will be expected of him."

"It must be a lot easier when a child is young like that because you can just tell them what to do and they have to do it."

Millie looked at her like she'd lost her mind. "I don't know anyone who has had a child like that, autism or no autism. And, if a child is that compliant, I'd worry about him." She continued. "I think some people would say the opposite of what you just did, that as their child grows older, it's easier because the child can reason for themselves and has more understanding. Little kids are quite self-centered, don't you find? It's only with age and maturity that they gain the ability to see someone else's perspective and actually care about the other person's position. Is that where Suzie is now?"

"Oh, no, not at all. In fact, I think it's gotten worse over the last few years." She put down her cup and faced Millie directly. "Do you know what she did this week?" She didn't wait for Millie's response. "I work every day, well five days a week. I'm tired. It's demanding work, and I'm always at the beck and call of others, sorting out problems, smoothing things over. By the end of the day, I'm beat. But, I have to go to the supermarket for us. Then I have to go home and make supper. You'd think that by now Suzie would get with the program and offer to bring in the groceries or put them away while I make our meal. What I wouldn't give to come home to a meal all ready and waiting for me. But, none of that happens."

"What does your daughter do? Have you tried asking her for help?"

"Have I? You'd think I was asking her to build a bridge or do something that will require fourteen hours of work. Just getting her to put her dishes in the dishwasher is a major battle, let alone getting her to empty that dishwasher. I'm surprised you haven't heard some of our fights all the way over here."

Millie didn't comment.

"It's just not worth it. I spend more time fighting with Suzie to get her to do something than it takes me to do the job myself. It's easier for both of us if I just do it."

"Is it better for you? For either of you?"

"Yes, when all I long for is a bit of peace."

"I see."

"I notice other mothers out enjoying themselves with their daughters. They shop. They go for coffee, for dinner, they do stuff and they like being with each other, sharing things. But, it's not like that with Suzie and me.

"I love my daughter, don't get me wrong. And I'm sure that on some level she loves me, too. But it's just that our relationship feels so unequal, with me doing all the work. That makes me sound awfully selfish, doesn't it?"

"Not at all. No one likes things to go all one way. We suffer through that when kids are babies because we know that period will only last a short while. Then things become more reciprocal and there is give and take, depending on the age of the child. By the time our offspring reach adulthood, we expect a more equal blend of give and take."

"Well, it didn't work that way in my case. We've gone backward, if anything."

"What does your daughter say when you ask her for help?"

"She feels I'm interrupting her work and anything she's doing is more important than what I want her to do."

"Maybe it's true some of the time. I know that Kyle concentrates intensely when he's doing something he likes. It can be hard to get his attention. Mel gives him warnings of when something must end, rather than expecting him to just suddenly stop."

"And does he? Stop, I mean?"

Millie grinned. "That depends. Yes, it's getting better, better all the time. That's mostly because Mel won't stand for anything else. She does not let him have his way, but she does give times when he gets to do just what he wants, but within limits. She says that kids with autism can get too into themselves. They need time to pursue their own interests and spend time the way they want but it must be kept within limits. And, she does not allow that to interfere with their family time, nor with his chores."

"Chores? Kyle has chores? He's just a kid."

"Of course, he has chores. He lives here, doesn't he? Everyone has to contribute to the smooth running of a household. It only makes sense, plus it's good training. He's learning responsibility and that people depend on him and he feels part of things around here."

"He must be a strange kid if he likes to do chores."

"Oh, lord love a duck. Did I give you the impression that Kyle likes doing chores? Mercy, no. I'm surprised you haven't heard some of the battles, well they were rather one-sided battles. Kyle yelled and Mel waited. Ben and I were ready to tantrum as well, but Mel just waits out the storm, then points to the job that Kyle was supposed to do."

"And he just does it?"

"Now, yes. But in the beginning, oh, no. Sometimes it would start up all over again, with him bellowing and hollering and Mel waiting. She wouldn't let him go do what he wanted until his job was done."

"That does not sound like fun."

"Nope, it wasn't, not for anyone. But we had to weather those storms to get to where we are now."

"How did Mel insist?"

"She has these cards she made that she laminated. There's the word 'First' with a space, then the word, 'Then'. She either draws a picture or writes the word of the chore in the first space and a picture or word of what Kyle wants to do in the 'Then' spot. And she stuck to it until Kyle got the idea."

"And that's it?"

"Huh. It sounds simple now, but it didn't feel that way at the time. And, he's a kid. Sometimes he still tries to slide out of things, but we try hard to stick to the rules."

"What kind of things does a kid his age have to do?"

"He sets the table for us for supper each night. He always puts his own dishes in the dishwasher. He empties the cutlery from the dishwasher. He feeds and waters our dog."

"Wow, that's a lot." Then in a smaller voice, "Suzie doesn't do nearly that much and never without a major protest."

"Oh, that's not all Kyle does. Saturday mornings, before he watches cartoons, he strips the sheets and pillowcase off his bed. That mainly looks like giving things a hard pull, balling them up and throwing them in the washing machine, but it gets the job done. He's allowed to watch two cartoons, and then he vacuums the living room floor."

"Wow."

"Oh, that vacuum sometimes zips around fast, and I'm not always sure if he's scattering the dust or sucking it up, but it's mostly all right. If his job is too sketchy, he has to come back and do it again. And, his jobs change. If he complains that he doesn't want to do something, he still has to do it, but then is offered a say in deciding the job he could do to replace that chore. He used to dust and Ben did the vacuuming in the living room, but they swapped jobs at Kyle's request. The deal is that he can trade jobs, but he still has to do a job."

"Well, I'm screwed. I didn't start that when Suzie was little, so it's too late now."

Millie's head tilted to one side. "Why?"

"It's easier to make a seven year old do something than it is to force a twenty-one year old."

"A young adult has reasoning powers that a child doesn't possess. Can't you talk to Suzie?"

"Talk? I talk 'til I'm blue in the face. She doesn't listen; doesn't want to listen. She just wants to do what she wants to do. You know, she has never once in her entire life pushed the buttons on a washing machine, let alone put her own clean clothes away."

Puzzled, Mille asked, "Why are you doing her laundry?"

"Honestly, she'd never have any clean underwear if I didn't."

"So?"

"So, you can't go around in dirty clothes."

"Does Suzie like having clean clothes?"

"She hates stains. If she spills some food on her shirt, she immediately rushes off to change."

"What happens to that dirty shirt then?"

"It goes in the laundry hamper and I wash it on the weekend."

"Hmm."

"What?" defensively.

"I'm not sure why you're doing her laundry. If she likes having clean clothing and she's old enough to run the washer and she's home all the time, why can't she do it herself? And do yours as well."

"She's never done it."

Millie looked at her a moment, then patted her hand. "Forgive me, dear, but I'm going to say this anyway. Whose fault is it that she's never done it?"

"Mine? Hers? Asperger's? It's because she has Asperger's that we have all these problems."

"You might want to have a chat with Mel about that. She has some strong ideas along this line. She says that autism or Asperger's explains the way a person might perceive the world or respond to the world initially. But it does not define that person. And, she strongly believes that having an autism spectrum disorder is not an excuse for bad behavior."

"I don't know if I'd call what Suzie does as bad behavior." Then Amanda paused and thought about what she'd just said. "Can I take that back? Yeah, some of it, maybe a lot of it looks like bad behavior." She sipped her now cold tea. "But what do I do about it now?"

"She's twenty-one, not a hundred and one. There's lots of time for her to learn new skills. She might not be a happy camper, but from the sounds of it she is not now and neither are you. All you're doing is asking her to help out around the house and to take some responsibility for herself. That is not too much to ask of anyone."

"She really won't like it."

"Does that matter? You don't like the way things are, but you're doing the stuff anyway. I don't know anyone who gets to only do the things she likes. There's stuff we just do because it has to get done. Isn't that part of what growing up is about?"

"Suzie is not used to that."

"She can get used to it. Listen, dear. If you carry on the way you're going, are you doing your child a favor? Are you preparing her for life?"

Amanda walked around the block before heading home. The evening air and her talk with Millie cleared her head somewhat. It was so easy to get stuck in a rut.

When had she and Suzie developed this pattern of being together? Once the imposed structure of going to school every day was gone, life seemed to become harder for Suzie. She didn't get up at the same time each morning anymore. She didn't leave the house. She didn't have work she had to hand in. Even though she had hated school, at least it was something to do and she wasn't so in to herself.

Amanda thought that Suzie used to help a bit around the house, or at least it wasn't a battle royal when she was asked to help with the dishes. The more Amanda had let her off the hook for sharing with household responsibilities, the less Suzie did. Amanda had assumed that as an adult, Suzie would just notice the things that needed to be done and do them. But that had not happened.

Then the anxiety got worse. In response, Amanda did more for Suzie, feeling sorry for her. But that hadn't helped, not really. The less Suzie did, the more she hid and the more the anxiety surfaced whenever she had to leave the house or do anything, almost anything at all.

Now, they were no longer just treading water, but they were sinking. Fast.

Suzie seemed unable to pull herself out of this slump. As her mother, it was Amanda's duty to help her, even if Suzie resisted, kicking and screaming all the way. If she could not find her way out of this mire on her own, her mother would have to light the way for her.

But how? And, were either of them strong enough to survive the journey?

CHAPTER 9

Much of the time growing up, Amanda had believed her brother was a pest at best, an idiot at worst. She was the sensible one, the one people could rely on, while he goofed off and generally enjoyed himself.

He had grown up, sure, but in her mind, he was still her kid brother. That's why she hated it when he was right.

She didn't like a lot of what he said about Suzie and he had no business criticizing how she raised her kid, but he did have some points. Even if he didn't get what life was like for Suzie, he had her best interests at heart and knew that she was going nowhere fast. And, in his own way, Amanda knew that her sibling loved her and was worried about her. With him, Amanda didn't try to hide her fatigue. He was family and there was no need to pretend around him.

She conceded that Todd was right, well, at least partially right. So she spent her lunch hour making a list.

Trying to be fair, she separated out breakfast and lunch duties. She and Suzie ate those meals alone. Her paper stipulated that after having breakfast or lunch, each person must either rinse her dishes and place them in the dishwasher or wash them by hand, leaving them to dry on the drying rack. Anything left on that rack must be put back in the cupboard before it was time to prepare the next meal. The same rules applied to any snacks made in the evening or nighttime.

Rereading what she'd written, Amanda thought those were simple rules to keep. Suzie would not. But, that was the easy stuff.

They'd ease gradually into the equal distribution of chores; Amanda was not up to battling World War Three, nor did she have the energy to enforce all the needed rules and impose the consequences for the likely infractions.

No, she'd start simpler.

Amanda would continue to be the cook in the house. She'd make each evening meal. And, she'd do all the grocery shopping.

But, each afternoon Suzie would need to empty the dishwasher, putting the clean dishes away. Before Amanda got home to make supper, Suzie would set the table. On the days Amanda brought home groceries, Suzie would put them away and do it immediately so that Amanda could prepare supper.

Mercy, this was going to be tough. Looking at this from an outside perspective, these were not onerous chores for a twenty-one year old. Most ten year olds could do this, thought Amanda. Maybe eight year olds.

Then, why wasn't Suzie? Did parents set these things up or did kids imitate on their own, following a parent's lead, wanting to help out? Amanda could not remember a time, even when Suzie was little, when she'd copied what Amanda was doing or tried to join in. Was that a feature of autism? Even as a toddler, Suzie was just as happy playing on her own and didn't seem to need to interact with her mother or her father. Sometimes she'd tolerate their presence and interference in her play, but more often than not, she'd turn her back and attempt to continue doing things her own way.

True, this was not uncommon in kids with autism. But because a kid had autism, did that mean that she had to stay the same? Suzie had changed lots in her lifetime. She'd gone from a screaming, tantrumming toddler to a, well, to a....

This week was not a good example. Suzie had learned to hold it together much of the time and was actually well-behaved when she was in school. Her teachers found her quiet and not a problem.

When she came home from school, it was often a different matter. Amanda thought that Suzie tried so hard to hold it together all day in school that she had to release the tension at home. And, her mother was the frequent brunt of those releases. But, they'd weathered them and over the years, they'd worked out a system that allowed them to live together mostly amicably.

How had they done that? Ruefully, Amanda wondered about the "they" and if it was more of she, Amanda, bending the world to that which suited Suzie. When she allowed herself to think about it truthfully, Amanda admitted that life was calmest for them when Suzie was free to do whatever she wanted. When demands were put on her, life became unpleasant for both of them. It was just easier to do all the work herself; keeping their home life calm. The other night had not been calm. Nope, not at all. But Amanda could have calmed things down; all she needed to do was back down and say they could continue on as they were.

Todd, that rotter, had planted the seeds in Amanda's mind that things needed to change. Had he really? No, those thoughts had been peeking their way towards Amanda's consciousness all on their own, but she'd been firmly tamping them down, knowing that if she allowed them to surface, she'd lose any peace they'd achieved in their house.

Todd simply gave her the nudge that she needed, that Suzie needed as well, if only she knew it. So, tonight was the night.

Amanda checked the rest of her list. She'd tried to think about things Suzie needed to be able to do on her own; things other girls her age did for themselves. One thing she thought she'd start with was laundry. From now on, they'd each be responsible for their own. Up to now, Amanda had done her own, then a load for Suzie separately. Not anymore. Now, Suzie would need to do her own.

Also on the list were a variety of other household things that needed to be done, which had been done only by Amanda up to now. These weren't difficult or time-consuming things, just those pesky chores that needed to be done weekly, like dusting, vacuuming, washing the kitchen floor, cleaning the bathroom, watering the plants and cutting the grass.

They'd divide these things up evenly; Suzie would get to choose whose name fell under each task. Easy, peasy, right? Right, as long as Amanda stuck to her guns. In the past she'd thrown away her backbone in the midst of Suzie's tantrums. Suzie was not stupid; she'd learned to be a good master of her environment. To be fair, she likely did what she did to keep herself calm.

In bending over backwards to keep her daughter happy, Amanda admitted that she may not have done Suzie a favor. Suzie was content, but ill prepared for life. Well, that was about to change. Tonight.

"Suzie, I'm home." Amanda waited. "Suzie?" She rapped on the basement door, and then opened it. "Suzie, come set the table now, please, and see what I brought."

She'd splurged. Suzie's favorite Vietnamese food was peanut chicken, pho soup and salad with crunchy, colorful shrimp chips. Call her chicken, but Amanda wanted a nice, peaceful supper before she brought out what she'd come to think of as 'The List'.

Slow footsteps trudged up the stairs. One look at Suzie's sullen face told Amanda that yes, Suzie had found the note she'd left, the note reminding Suzie that tonight they'd discuss divvying up the chores. Suzie entered the kitchen, bringing storm clouds with her. Amanda turned her back, pretending not to notice.

"Suzie, set the table, will you, please, while I get out the food."

A glance over her mom's shoulder told Suzie what was on the menu. She complied, setting the plates on the table with more force than needed, but the task got done and the china remained in one piece.

"Napkins too, please. I always drip those soup noodles on my chin. And I'd rather not wear them on this beige skirt."

Amanda chatted on about her day. She'd learned to hold up her side of the conversation even when her daughter asked no questions about Amanda's stories, nor added any comments or insights. Why would she? What Amanda was doing did not seem to interest Suzie. And, when Suzie talked about things that filled her with passion, she required no input from anyone else, and no help in keeping her recitations going. Amanda hadn't thought about it much before. Was that an autism thing? Did it have to be that way? Amanda was used to it and Todd had adapted to this one-sided way of conversing with Suzie. But, how would other people react? So far, that had been a moot question.

Trying to draw Suzie out, Amanda asked her about her day. "I worked."

"Oh, what did you work on?"

"My music and my rendering."

"How's it coming?"

"Fine."

Well, as far as conversations go, there was some back and forth, but not much else. Social niceties aside, maybe it was time to tackle the immediate issues.

Amanda pushed her plate and bowl to the side. Leaning over, she drew papers from her purse.

"I worked on this over lunch hour and have drawn up that list of chores I told you about."

"I'm not doing it."

Ignoring that, Amanda turned the pages so that they faced her daughter.

"I've divided this into two categories. The first page are things that we'll each do on our own. Some of these things are for ourselves and some are for our mutual benefit since we live together.

"Look here." She pointed to the breakfast and lunch headings. "Since we each eat these two meals on our own, we won't change anything about how we prepare or eat at these times."

Suzie's shoulders lost some of their tension.

"I'll continue to make enough for supper so that there should be leftovers for you for lunch. You'll eat that whenever you want and since we eat breakfast at different times, that won't change either. After each of us finishes either of these meals, we'll do one of two things, and the choice is yours. One, rinse your dirty dishes and place them in the dishwasher. Or two, wash those dishes by hand and place them in the drying rack. If you choose that option, those dishes must be put back in the cupboard before it's time for me to make supper. And, the dishwasher must be emptied by the time I'm home from work and ready to cook supper. If you choose option one, to place your dirty breakfast or lunch dishes in the dishwasher, you'll have to make sure that you've first emptied it and put all the clean dishes away. We usually run the dishwasher after supper, but if you think there's a better time, I'm open to suggestions."

"I don't like touching dirty dishes. You know that. They're gross. They look ugly and they smell."

"I agree. They are gross. But dirty dishes are a fact of life. Everybody has to take care of them."

"I don't."

Amanda looked quickly at her daughter. She was right, at least right up to now.

"You haven't done them very often in the past, that's true. But it's no longer true. From now on I'll cook supper and you clean up afterwards."

Suzie's arms folded and her lip came out. Was that an honest to god pout on her adult child's face? Oh, this talk was so long overdue.

"There is another possibility," Amanda offered. "If you'd prefer, I will clean up the kitchen after you cook our meal."

"I can't cook, you know that."

"Hmm. Maybe it's time you learned."

"No!"

"No? Well, if you like to eat, you have to cook. But we can get to that a little later, if you'd like. For now, if it's your choice that I do the cooking, then your part in the arrangement is to clean up."

"Why do we have to change anything? We're doing all right now." She looked around the kitchen. "The place looks all right."

"Yes, it does but that's because I cleaned it. There are two adults living in this house and only one adult doing the work. That is changing now. We're sharing this living space and we're sharing the job of looking after it."

Suzie plopped back in her chair, slouched and looked away.

"So, we're each looking after our own breakfast and lunch, I'm making supper and you're cleaning up the kitchen after supper and taking care of the dishwasher.

"I'll continue to do the grocery shopping, unless you'd rather take that on?" She waited. When there was no response, she continued. "Okay, I'll get the groceries. I'll let you know when I arrive home with them. You'll bring them in and put them away while I work on supper."

Suzie opened her mouth to protest, but Amanda held up a finger to cut her off.

"And, I need your input on this. I always get the groceries, buying what I want. I can't think of the last time I asked you if there was anything in particular you wanted. I'm sorry about that. So, from now on, this goes on the refrigerator." She held up a pad of paper fastened to a magnet. She placed the unit on the fridge. "This is where we'll keep our weekly grocery list and each of us can add whatever we need to it. This will also help me be more organized. Some weeks I'm stopping at the supermarket three or four times a week, running in for things I've forgotten. This list should help and save time. So, add whatever you think we should have on hand, or write down things when you notice we're running low. And, see this box at the bottom? I'd like you to write down meals or dishes that you might like to have that week. I find it hard to come up with dinner ideas. I'll cook it if you can tell me what you'd like. It occurred to me that you pretty much eat what I come up with and you don't have much say into our evening meals. Well, that will change now and you get to have more input. Sound okay?"

Suzie nodded, but watched her mother warily.

So far, so good. The protests had been mostly token, she thought.

"Now, this next section on the list is stuff we'll each do for ourselves. I'll clean my room, the entryway and the outside deck. You'll be responsible for your bedroom and the basement; you're the only one who goes down there much."

At Suzie's look of horror, Amanda amended, "I don't mean the entire downstairs, just the living area with the couches and computer." Suzie eased back into her slump.

"We'll also each be responsible for our own laundry. That means our clothes, sheets and towels. So we're not fighting for the washing machine at the same time, I thought I'd take Saturday morning as the time I'll do my laundry. Does that suit you?"

"But I don't know how to do laundry. You always do that; all my life you've done that. I don't even know how to use those machines."

"Oh, they're a cinch. Given your techie skills, it'll be nothing for you to learn. Throw in the soap, push a button and you're good to go."

"I'm too busy. I don't have time to fiddle around with that."

Amanda regarded her daughter steadily. Did Suzie seriously think her mother had more spare time than she, the unemployed, stay-at-home adult child? "Suzie, we no longer need to beat our clothes with a rock at the stream or use a scrub board by hand. It takes less than three minutes to throw a load into the washing machine and push the button. The machine does all the work for you. Then, another minute or so to transfer the clothes from the washing machine to the dryer and push another button. In the half hour or so the machines are doing their thing, you go do your thing."

"What if I'm too busy? What if I don't remember?"

"Well, you might have to wear dirty underwear."

At Suzie's look of horror, she added, "Maybe you could turn your underwear inside out and wear it that way until you have time to do a load of laundry." Oh, it was not nice to tease your child. Was it? "Tell me when you're ready to do your first load and I'll show you how to use the machines."

"I'm not good with directions and lectures. You know that. What if I forget?"

"Good point. I'll write out the directions for each machine and tape them to the wall by the washer. Okay?"

No response, then, a quiet voice muttered, "It would be easier if you just did it."

Perhaps it would, in many ways. But it would not be better for Suzie, if only she knew it.

"Next is this second page. Here I've made a list of common chores that have to be done around the house. On the left side here I've listed the weekly chore, and then there are two more columns, one for each of us. I'll get to that in a minute.

"Here's the list: vacuum the living room, dust the living room, cut the grass, wash the kitchen floor, clean the bath tub, clean the toilet, clean the bathroom sink, wash the bathroom floor. These are the things we'll start with for now."

"For now! Those things will take forever to do!"

"Actually, they don't and I know that from experience. I know that the list looks long, but these are not all things you have to do. I'll be doing half of them. I want you to take this list and divide it up equally between the two of us, four items each. Beside each task, write down when you think it should be done. I don't care if you think we should go on a cleaning blitz each Saturday morning or if you think these things should be spaced out over the week. You decide. Just make sure that we each have four things to do and that you've marked down when they must be done by."

Suzie snatched up the paper. "I am absolutely not ever, ever, ever cleaning a toilet. That is so gross. You can't make me." She threw the paper at her mother.

"Fine, if you don't want to clean the toilet right now, add that under my list. But young lady, you will clean a toilet in your life. Everyone has to, or else things get really gross."

"I don't have time to be piddling around with stuff like this. Do you know how much time this crap will take?"

"Actually I have a very good idea of exactly how much time each of these things takes. I do them all the time. Remember? And, I'm gone from the house over fifty hours each week. Yet, somehow I've found time to get all these things done. No more, though. We are going to share in looking after this house."

"That's what you think. You know how I can't take pressure. My anxiety goes crazy; I can feel it now. My blood pressure's probably high, too, from all this stress. How can you do this to me? You're my mother; you're supposed to care about me, to help me. Instead, you're ruining my life." Suzie snatched up the papers and tore them in half again and again, watching her mother defiantly.

Amanda carefully kept her face neutral. When Suzie was done and had sprinkled the confetti on the kitchen table, Amanda reached into her purse, pulling out duplicate copies of the lists. She knew her daughter and had come prepared. She'd hoped for a more mature reaction, but was ready, just in case. She held the new copy out to Suzie.

"Here. Go through the list and by morning I expect to see your name by four tasks and my name by four and the time/day when each needs to be done."

"Right." When did Suzie learn to be sarcastic?

"If you decide not to divide up the list for us by morning, then I'll do it for us." She held up a third copy of the list. "But, I'll give you first choice." Her voice steeled. "You will do four of these tasks each week and I will do four. That is not optional. What is optional is which of the four you choose to do and when you choose to do them. But I will hold you to the times you said you'd do them. And, you can hold me to my word; I will do the tasks you pick for me at the times you feel best."

Suzie's arms were crossed again. "And if I don't?"

She met Suzie's eyes. "There will be a consequence. That's how life works. Remember that old saying, 'First we work, then we play'? Well, the chore must be done before privileges are allowed."

"Privileges? What privileges do I get?"

Oh, how had she ever raised such a spoiled child? She could hear Todd's 'I told you so' ringing in her ears. "People earn their privileges. Watching television is a privilege, eating take-out food is a privilege, using a computer is a privilege as is all the other technology you use."

Suzie's hands flapped at her side. She rocked back and forth, and then her hands curled into fists. "That's my computer! You can't touch it! That's my life and you have no right to go near it."

CHAPTER 10

Todd's car was in the driveway when Amanda got home from work. Carrying as many grocery bags as she could in one trip, she made her way to the kitchen. As she approached the back step, the door was flung open and Todd reached for her bags. The aroma of hot, cheesy pizza filled her senses.

"What are you doing here?" she asked. Her nose sniffed the tantalizing scents.

Suzie was at the counter tossing the makings for a Caesar salad. Amanda stopped short when she saw this activity. "I didn't know you knew how to make a salad."

"Uncle Todd taught me. It's not that hard."

Was that all it took, wondered Amanda? She's been tossing the salads for years on her own. How had Todd managed to get Suzie to help out?

Todd began emptying the bags. "Suzie, I don't know where most of this stuff goes. I'll put it on the counter and you stash it in the proper places while your mom washes up."

To Amanda's amazement, Suzie got to work alongside her uncle. Well, don't look a gift horse in the mouth and all that. She went down the hallway, grateful to strip off her work duds and get into comfortable old jeans and a sweatshirt. The better to drip pizza sauce on, she thought.

Supper was fun, actually fun. Todd kept all of them laughing with his stories. Suzie was relaxed and seemed to eat without thinking about it. This was a far cry from the silent, tense meals they'd shared this past week. Maybe the problem was her approach, Amanda thought. Did she attack her daughter, trying to get her to help out? Todd joked and cajoled and made it all seem natural and fun.

After they'd all eaten as much as they could and the spumoni ice cream bucket was starting to melt, Todd stood and organized them. "Here, Suzie. I'll hand you the dishes and you put them in the dishwasher. Amanda, you handle the ice cream."

When she finished her part, Amanda looked around for the next thing to do. Todd shooed her away. "Get, go on. We've got this. You go get ready."

"Ready?"

"Yeah, your big date. Go."

Suzie's head jerked up. "What are you talking about?"

Amanda looked confused. "What are you talking about, Todd."

Now Todd's brow wrinkled. "Tonight's the day you're going out with that guy, the one who called when I was here before. And, more importantly, tonight's the day I make Suzie wish she'd never seen a Scrabble board."

"But I'm not going anyplace. What on earth would make you think I had a date?"

"Yeah," Suzie agreed. "Mom doesn't date."

Todd looked between the two of them. "Mandy, you didn't turn the guy down, did you? I told you I'd be here and that Suzie and I would be fine when you went out."

"I just," Amanda hesitated, not wanting to say much in front of Suzie.

"Well, go call him now," Todd urged. "You officially have a night off. Go. Get."

"I already told him I couldn't and besides, I don't know his number."

Todd strode to their phone and scrolled through the call history. "Would this be it?"

Amanda shrugged and pretended not to know.

"Suzie, wipe off the table while I grab the Scrabble board." When Amanda grabbed a third chair to join in, Todd stopped her. "Nope, no you don't. This night is for Suzie and me, right Suzie? Just me and my favorite niece."

"Uncle Todd, I'm your only niece."

"That doesn't mean you can't be my favorite."

"But, I don't have anything else planned," started Amanda.

"Tough. That's your problem. You had your opportunity, now scram. Suzie and I need to concentrate."

Amanda wandered into the living room. She picked up the remote but nothing on the television grabbed her interest. Most of her attention was on the snatches of conversation she could hear from the kitchen and the occasional burst of laughter. They seemed to be having a good time - everyone else was enjoying themselves. Well, she'd wanted time to just relax. Now that she had it, why did it not seem quite so welcome? Her gaze strayed to the phone. Could she?

When had she last been on a date? Hmm. That was twenty-some years ago. Back then, she'd been a shy, insecure girl, certainly not forward and most definitely she had never asked a boy out on a date.

Times had changed, though. Woman did more things, took more initiative. Could she call Jack?

Amanda picked up a pillow and hugged it to her chest. What was the upside of trying? Maybe she'd get to know Jack a bit more, maybe she'd have some fun with him, maybe she'd forget her cares for just a little while and maybe, just maybe, her brother Todd would not be the only man in her life.

But was that fair to Jack? She was not free to be anything more than a friend, a person to spend some time with on those rare occasions when Suzie was all right to be left on her own. Would Jack want more that she was able to give him?

And now for the downside of attempting to call Jack. Amanda had to admit that as embarrassed as she sometimes felt at work, it was rather flattering to have a man show such obvious interest in her. She's not felt chased since Dwayne tried to woo her all those years ago. Several decades plus a failed marriage later, it felt good to have some man find her attractive. And, not just any man. Jack was in no way anyone's left-overs. Amanda noticed the admiring glances other women in the office tossed Jack's way. But, he never seemed to notice. When he came into the building, he headed straight for her desk, his face beaming when their eyes met. Even her gentle discouraging ways had not dissuaded him and Jack still kept coming back.

His phone calls in the evening were nice. Nice. Amanda hated to admit to herself just how much she looked forward to them.

But, he'd not called once so far this week. Had she finally succeeded in putting him off for good? A part of Amanda had hoped to accomplish just that; she did not have the time in her life nor the energy to be involved in a relationship. If he wanted more, was it not fair to this nice man that she cut things off before they really started? Yes, that was the sensible thing to do, the fair thing, best for both Jack and for Suzie.

Amanda lay back on the couch, still snuggling with the pillow and tried to get into the intricacies of the television characters' competitions on the island SURVIVOR.

Commercials left just too much time to think. They interrupted Amanda's boob tube trance and gave her time to ponder her life. Yuk. Nothing good came of excess introspection, she told herself.

Tempted as she might be, Amanda could not call Jack. She'd never asked him for his phone number, had not even considered that request when he had asked for hers.

Ah, the show was back on. Amanda allowed herself to get sucked back into the trials and tribulations of island tribes and alliances.

Were television episodes shorter than they used to be? It seemed only minutes ago that she watched the last batch of commercials.

While her conscious mind weighed the pros of certain laundry detergents, her fingers acted with a will of their own. They drew her eyes to the cordless phone screen and the call history numbers scrolled by. There. That one. It appeared every so often and didn't belong to her family or any business she remembered calling.

What would happen if she pressed dial? If it was a company, she'd get no answer or a recording and she could hang up. And if it was anyone else, she could still hang up anyway, couldn't she?

"Hello?"

Rats. Now what did she do?

"Hello?" A pause, then, "Amanda, is that you?"

Damn technology. He must have looked at her number. In a voice she hardly recognized, she admitted, "Yes, it's me, Amanda."

The warmth rushed into Jack's voice. "I'm so glad you called. How are you?"

"I'm fine. And you?" Oh, how inane could her conversation get? Think, think, think. What was she going to say when he asked why she was calling? She could hardly say that it was her wayward fingers, not her.

"I'm so glad you called, Amanda. I was worried that I'd been bugging you too much, taking too much of your time, so decided I should give you some space."

"I decided it should be my turn to call this time."

She could hear the pleasure in his voice. "Sure, we could take turns. You know, when I first heard your voice, I wondered if you'd changed your mind and were going to invite me over tonight."

Amanda hesitated. Should she? Could she? Maybe she waited too long, because Jack broke in before she could marshal her thoughts.

"Sorry, I don't mean to be so forward. It's getting late and you're probably tired after working all week. I wouldn't mind having a chat though. Sometimes this house gets a bit lonely at night."

Then, the awkwardness was over and they talked the way they had other evenings, about everything and nothing, sharing a joke and lifting each other's spirits. But through all their easy camaraderie, they never touched on those heavy topics, those near to their hearts. It was from secretaries in the office that Amanda learned that Jack was a widower, having lost his wife to breast cancer several years ago. And as for her, well, Amanda had hinted that her situation was difficult but she had not elucidated on just what it was that made things burdensome for her.

Burdensome. Was that how she saw Suzie, as a burden? To be honest, sometimes. What an awful thing for a mother to feel, a mother who loved her child more than life. Suzie needed her. Suzie had special needs. It was not Suzie's fault that she had Asperger's Syndrome. Amanda was responsible and she would live up to her responsibilities.

CHAPTER 11

Amanda's thoughts must have led to an awkward pause in their conversation. Jack cleared his throat. "Amanda, I don't want you to think I was gossiping about you or even asking things behind your back. But, I couldn't help but hear in the coffee room talk about autism and Asperger's Syndrome and that you had a child with Asperger's. Is that true?"

Amanda's shoulders slumped. Were her pleasant interludes with Jack now over? Was this a deal breaker and he'd want no more time with her, knowing that any relationship with such a mother was a dead end?

Jack continued. "I really hope you don't take this the wrong way."

Here is comes, thought Amanda.

"I don't want to interfere in any way. I just wanted to understand and to help if there was ever anything I could do. So, I started reading. I read a bunch of stuff on the internet. Some of it was confusing and over my head, especially the neurology stuff. And some of what I read, especially in forums was negative. Some of it seemed just wrong. But there was other stuff that seemed hopeful. I liked the stuff written by young adults who have Asperger's who wrote about how they were finding their way and the things that helped them. I found some books they mentioned and ordered them.

"I've been reading and I've started to get a bit of a handle on what it might be like to have Asperger's." His voice became more eager. "There's this book that was written by a boy when he was just thirteen years old - Luke Jackson. The book's called, Freaks, Geeks and Asperger's Syndrome."

When Amanda didn't reply, he hurried on. "Please don't be insulted by that title. I don't think Luke meant anything bad by it. You see, he has Asperger's himself and he has a brother with autism. I love this kid's attitude. He writes openly about the things that are hard for him, and then he talks about the strategies he uses to make his way. He sounds like a pretty together kid, well he did then anyway. He must be an adult now. Amanda? Amanda, have you read his book?"

"No."

"Do you not enjoy reading?"

"No, I like it fine. I just feel too tired lately and it's easier to veg out in front of the TV."

"I hear you. I do that sometimes, too, but I thought it was important that I learn about this Asperger's thing and once I started looking into it, I found it fascinating."

"You wouldn't if you lived it day in and day out, believe me."

"I didn't mean to sound insensitive. It must be rough, both for you and for your daughter. But I've read so much hopeful stuff. Some of these kids find the social life in high school tough, but things get better for them after that. There are lots of kids with Asperger's doing well in college and getting jobs and living independent, productive lives. That must give you so much hope for when your child grows up. How old did you say she is?"

"Twenty-one." There, she's admitted it.

"Oh. And what is she doing now?"

Silence.

"Amanda? Amanda, are you there?"

She could only nod as the tears rolled down her cheeks and clogged her throat. Slowly and gently, she set the phone back in its cradle and listened to the click that severed the connection.

There was the sound of feet pounding up the front steps, and then the door bell sounded. With only a couple seconds pause, it rang again and yet again.

From the kitchen, the murmur of Todd and Suzie's voices paused. "Amanda? Are you getting that?"

A fist began banging on the door. Amanda feigned sleep, propped on her side on the couch, hugging her pillow.

Todd sighed and said, "I'll get it." He glanced through the glazed sidelight and saw a wavy outline of a man's form. First ensuring that the safety chain was on, he opened the door a few inches. Immediately, the man pushed against the door, calling, "Amanda? Amanda are you all right?"

Todd stood back, glancing into the living room. "Mandy, do you know this guy?"

It was hard to pretend to be napping with all this racket. Amanda lifted her head. Her name was called again from outside the door. The man tried to insert his toe in the door and push. He put his one eye to the opening and asked Todd, "Who are you? What have you done to Amanda?" Then louder, "Amanda!"

Todd kept his shoulder firmly against the door. "Mandy, what's going on here?" To the man, he asked, "Who are you and how do you know my sister?"

"Your sister! Then she's all right? Where is she? We were talking on the phone and then there was just dead air. I called back immediately but couldn't get through on either her land line of her cell. I thought something had happened to her. Where is she? I need to see that she's all right."

"Sis, you better show yourself. Is it all right if I let this guy in?"

"Tell him I've gone to bed."

"Come on, Mand. The guy's standing right here. He can hear you. Do I let him in or not?"

As if she weighed far more than she did, Amanda heaved herself off the couch. She didn't even bother running her hands through her hair or try to flatten out the pillow creases on her cheek. What did it matter how she looked? Things were over anyway, over before they really even started. As she entered the hallway, she noticed her daughter's face peeking around the corner in the kitchen.

As Amanda approached the front door, Todd slid an arm around her shoulders. "How you doing, kid? You know this guy?"

Amanda nodded.

"Can I come in?" asked Jack. "I want to make sure you're all right."

Again, Amanda nodded.

Todd pushed the door shut, slid off the chain, and then opened the door all the way. He pulled Amanda back with him, still wary of this stranger who had pounded on the door.

The cool night air rushed in along with Jack. Ignoring Todd and his protective stance, he headed straight for Amanda, wrapped his arms around her and pressed her head to his shoulder. "I thought something had happened to you. I was so worried." He rubbed on hand gently up and down her back.

Amanda slumped against him. It had been some time since she enjoyed the comfort of a man's embrace. Gradually, where she was and how she looked penetrated her brain. She pulled back slightly, eyes on the middle button of Jack's shirt.

"Amanda?" he asked. "Tell me you're all right." Then he looked at Todd and his arm tightened around Amanda. "Are you afraid of this guy?" He glared at Todd.

Todd stepped back raising both hands, palm up at shoulder height. "Hey, buddy. Don't look at me that way. I wondered if you were okay." Then, turning to his sister, "Aren't you going to introduce us?"

"Um, yeah." Amanda stepped back, eyes lowered. "Todd, this is Jack. Jack, this is my brother, Todd."

Sizing each other up, the men shook hands. Jack offered, "I met Amanda at her office."

"Oh, you must be the guy on the phone. The one she can't go out with."

Jack's hackles rose again. "Why would you tell Amanda she can't go out with me?"

"Whoa. I said no such thing. I'm just repeating what Amanda told me when I asked her about it. She's a big girl and makes her own decisions. It's pretty obvious that I have no influence over her; I told her she should get out sometimes."

Jack placed a finger under Amanda's chin. "Look at me, please. Let me see that you're all right." When Amanda's eyes met his, he smiled. "So, did we have a bad connection and I panicked for nothing?"

Amanda shook her head.

"Did I say something that upset you?"

Amanda sighed. "No, it wasn't anything you said, but yes, I was upset. But it had nothing to do with you."

"What was it that upset you then?"

Amanda took a step back, a bit closer to Todd. "It's complicated. And, hard to explain."

Jack looked over at Todd.

"Don't look at me," said Todd. "I don't get it either."

Amanda looked out the corner of her eye toward the kitchen when there was a slight flash of a jean clad leg.

"Suzie, come on out here," called Todd. "You have company."

There was no response. Amanda put her hand on Todd's arm and started to speak.

Todd ignored her. "If the mountain won't come to Muhammad and all that." He motioned to Jack with his hand. "Come and meet the rest of the family." He led the way into the kitchen where Suzie was attempting to flee to the basement. "Hold it right there," Todd called to her. He went to Suzie and drew her tightly into his side. He turned them both to face Jack. "Jack I'd like to meet Suzie, Amanda's daughter. Suzie, this is your mother's friend, Jack."

Jack took a couple steps forward and held out his hand. "I'm pleased to meet you." He waited.

Suzie's face was turned toward her uncle's chest. Todd nudged her forward and half-turned her. "Suzie," he said. "The gentleman's trying to shake your hand." When she made no motion to reciprocate, he took her shoulders and turned her. "Go ahead." There was steel in his voice. Over her head, his eyes met those of his sister. His gaze warned her not to interfere.

Eyes downcast, Suzie raised her hand a few inches and allowed Jack to gently take it in his.

"Let's sit down, shall we?" Todd drew the chairs around the kitchen table. "Mand, is there any of that tea left?"

"I'll make some more."

An awkward silence descended. Trying, Jack said, "Looks like this was a pretty good Scrabble game. Who won?"

"Suzie did, as usual. But we were about to have a rematch."

"Great. May I join in? Looks like there's four of us." He looked over his shoulder at Amanda. "Do you play, too?"

"No!" This came from Suzie.

Jack turned to her. "Your mother doesn't play Scrabble?"

"No. I mean, yes she does, but we only ever play two at once. Either mom and me or Uncle Todd and me. You can't play."

"Suzie!" Her mother was horrified.

"We've played the three of us before," added Todd.

"Yes, but that's just us. Just family. No one else."

"What's with you, Suzie?" asked Todd.

"We don't know him. He doesn't belong here with us."

Amanda's hand covered her mouth as if she would have liked to place that hand across her daughter's lips. Todd glanced at her, anger in his voice. "Why are you being so rude to your mother's guest? Apologize. Now."

"That's all right. She wasn't expecting me to just burst into here tonight, unannounced. It'll take time for her to feel comfortable with me. But we'll get to be great friends, won't we Suzie?" Jack smiled, trying to look as nonthreatening as possible.

Suzie stood. "No. We won't be friends and I won't be getting to know you. Don't think you can worm your way in here. It's just mom and me, has been since I was a little girl and that's the way it'll always be. We have a good thing going, mom and me and you're not wrecking it." She turned and ran down the stairs.

The silence that fell over the rest of the group was beyond awkward.

Trying to ease the tension, Jack said, "Seems she takes her Scrabble games pretty seriously. I'm guessing she was never much for surprise parties either."

Todd's expression was about as angry as Amanda had ever seen him. He put one elbow on the table and gestured with his hand toward the basement stairs where the sounds of Sara Bareilles's song, Brave blared. For a few seconds the three around the table listened to the lyrics. Todd shook his head. "I bet she doesn't even get the irony of her choice in music." He turned to Amanda. "So, is this what you want? This is what I've been trying to talk to you about. It's not healthy for her and it's certainly not healthy for you." He dumped the Scrabble tiles into the lid of the back and began turning them face down. "Let's play." He didn't ask; he told them.

Jack eased his chair away from the table. "Look, it's late. Sorry to have barged in on you uninvited. I see that I've disrupted your household and that was not my intention." He turned to Amanda and squeezed her hand. "Now that I know you're all right, I'd better be off."

"No," said Todd. "We're playing. And, we're going to have fun." He looked at Amanda and Jack defiantly. "Can't you see? We can't let her get away with this. She can't think she has the ability to chase you away." To Amanda, he added, "She can't rule the roost, Mandy. This has got to stop. You deserve to have a life and unless you make major changes around here, she's never going to have a life either. Now draw a tile."

Taking his cue from Amanda, Jack followed her and took a tile. "Looks like I get to go first."

"What kind of tea did you make," asked Todd.

"Just regular orange pekoe."

"Let's spice it up a bit. Anyone for blueberry tea?" He proceeded to add a dash of Grand Marnier and Amaretto to their cups.

Todd pushed back his chair. "Well, that's it for me. I'll go say good night to Suzie, and then I'm hitting the road."

Jack stood as well. "I should be going as well. I barged in and have likely outstayed my welcome."

Todd waved him back. "Nah, it's early. Stay. Amanda could use the company."

"Geez, Todd," Amanda protested. "You make me sound so needy."

He gave her a pointed look behind Jack's back.

Closing the basement door behind him, he descended into the almost darkness. Calling softly, he said, "Suzie, it's just me."

From near the darkened computer monitor came the sound of quiet sobbing.

"Ah, Suzie, honey," Todd said as he gathered her into his arms.

"Uncle Todd, I'm sorry. I made a fool of myself and embarrassed mom, but it's so hard." Suzie's words were muffled against his shirt.

Todd stroked her hair back from her face. "Talk to me, Suzie. What is it that's so hard?"

"Everything. What isn't? That guy upstairs must hate me. He'll think I'm such a brat. And mom must hate me, too."

"You know that your mom could never hate you, even when she's upset with you."

"I know what I did was wrong and sometimes I am such a brat. I'm just so scared all the time."

"What is it that makes you afraid?"

"What doesn't? I know I'm not like other people. I see what other girls my age do; they're on the TV and I watch them in the malls. They make it look so easy, so normal. But I can't do what they do; can't even imagine how to start being like them."

Todd made sympathetic noises, even though he didn't quite get it.

The words all came bubbling out now. "Mom is a good woman, but sometimes I'm so mean to her. I know it and I know that it hurts her. She thinks I can't tell, but I can see that sometimes she's really tired when she comes home from work. She wants me to help out more. A part of me knows that that is only fair, but another part of me is scared. What all will she ask of me? If I give in and do some things, will she start expecting more and more? What if I can't do it? Will she be too disappointed in me? Will she kick me out? Is all this leading up her getting rid of me?

"I can't live on my own, Uncle Todd, I know I just can't. It would be too hard. It feels like Mom's trying to push me and it's all too much, too fast. I need time to get my head around it.

"Some of the stuff she asks me to do does not seem like a big deal to her. But it is to me. Hours before she comes home from work, I start thinking about it. I think of the stuff she wants me to do and all the things that could go wrong. What if I made a mistake? She wants me to bring the groceries in from the car - in the dark, even. What if something falls out of the bag and I don't notice it in the corner of the trunk. What if it's an orange and it starts to rot in there? It would be so gross and stink up the car. It could attract insects and ants and mice and there'd be an infestation and they'd wreck the car and we don't have the money to buy a new one. Or what if I dropped the carton of eggs and some spilled in the car? The stink of rotten eggs would be there forever and we couldn't use the car. Or the same thing could happen with milk or cream or yogurt. We're not rich, Uncle Todd. I know mom doesn't have enough money to buy a new car if I wreck this one.

"Or, what if I have my head in the trunk and someone walks by and says something to me? If it's a neighbor, I should say something back but I suck at small talk. And how do I know if it's a neighbor, someone I should talk to or a stranger, a sleazy stranger I should avoid.

"And, last week when mom got out of the car, she stepped in dog poo from the guy next door's Rottweiler. Sometimes he's over here. I can't stand strong smells or squishy things. If I stepped in some of that I'd barf. I know I would, right there and all over our groceries. Then I'd probably pass out in it, face down in the puke and poop." Suzie shuddered and drew her hunched shoulders even farther into herself.

"Yeow, Suzie. That's a lot of worries wrapped up in one little head."

"That's only part of it, Uncle Todd, the part just this week." She raised her head to look directly at him. "What's going to become of me? I know that mom will not live forever, and then who will look after me? I hate being this dependent but not having mom to look after me, having to do all the things she does terrifies me. It's all too much. I couldn't do it. I'll die first." The crying started up again. "What's wrong with me? Why can't I be like other people? They finish high school, get a job, a place of their own or go away to college. I'm not stupid, I know I'm not, but I just can't imagine me doing any of those things. When I try to think about it, I get exhausted. My head hurts so much and I shake. Look at my hands." She held out her palms so he could see. There were four crescent shaped divots in each from clenching her fists so hard.

Todd took her hands, smoothing out her fingers. "Suzie, no one is going to expect from you more than you can give at the time. We love you honey and know that this is overwhelming for you. But, you're not happy with the way things are, are you?"

Suzie wouldn't meet his gaze.

He put a finger under her chin, lifting her eyes to her. "It's okay to be honest. We're not going to get anywhere if we're not honest with each other. We all care and want the best for each other, and that includes you. Now, can you honestly tell me that you like the way your life is shaping up?" He held his breath waiting for her answer.

She shook her head.

"So, we're all in agreement. Something must change and change for both you and for your mom. But we can talk about it. Change can come in little bits, without making you bite off more than you can handle. "

"I know that you hate change." He grinned. "You make that loud and clear." He hugged her. "Most of us are not fond of change because it's different and we may not know exactly how that change will work out. But change is a part of life and happens to all of us. You can't grow or move on without change. We won't ask more of you than you can do right now then, but we will ask things of you."

When there was no reply, Todd said in a softer voice, "We'll help you, Suzie. Your mom and I will be here every step of the way."

"And will that guy be here too?"

"Maybe. I don't know. But if not him, then it might be some other guy. Your mother is still a young woman and sometimes she must get lonely."

As Suzie started to protest, he held up a hand. "I know, I know, you're here. And I know that the two of you spend time together but how do most of your evenings go?"

"Sometimes we watch TV."

"But most of the time it's Amanda upstairs alone and you're down here on the computer. Right?"

"I guess. But, I like it. There is so much stuff to do and I'm learning things all the time."

"Honey, that's all right. We all need interests and hobbies and we should get to spend free time the way we want to. But the things that fascinate you don't interest your mom. Did you ever think that she might want a little adult conversation or someone to hang out with? What about someone to listen to how her day was or to talk over things that bother her?"

Suzie was silent.

"Maybe Jack will be just a friend; maybe he will become more to your mom. Don't you think she deserves a chance to find out? What if she never dates, then you move out and on with your life and she'll be here, old and alone. Is that the kind of life you want for her?"

"Like that is ever going to happen."

"You don't know that. Who knows what the next years might bring for you and for your mom?" Todd continued. "I want you to think about this. It seems to me that for the last while you've been focusing on what your mom can and should do for you. But I want you to think about what you should do for her. Sometimes even the little things can make a big difference. You may not realize it, but she needs you, too."

☐

CHAPTER 12

Amanda stirred. Was it the moon shining in her face that woke her? Maybe. Or, was it that creak? The house settled. It was an old house; it did that. Amanda flipped her pillow over and nuzzled it into the right position with her cheek. For a second, she watched a cloud float across the moon's haze, then drifted back to sleep.

There is was again, that creak. Her eye, the one not snuggled into the pillow, opened. Somehow, it was easier to listen with her eye open. Now, how did that work? She lifted her head off the down pillow so she could hear with both ears.

Suzie. That was it. Even though her bedside clock told her it was three forty-five, the middle of the night that was just late evening to Suzie. She'd be at that computer all night. Again. The bitter part of Amanda's brain thought how nice it would be to get to do whatever you wanted, pursue your interests instead of having to drag yourself out of bed to a job that had lost its shine years ago. But, someone had to support them and it sure as heck wouldn't be Suzie anytime soon. She settled back into sleep.

Who knew how much longer it was until yet another noise woke her. She knew that squeak. It was the knob of the basement door. She heard the quiet click of the latch opening. There was a pause, a long pause. What was Suzie doing? Usually she tripped up the stairs faster than that. And, she always closed the door behind her. She did not want anyone to see what she was doing on her computer or in her drawing projects. There. That was the sound of the door closing again. Suzie was up making herself some food. She cooked, of a sort; she had to since her schedule was so out of sync with the rest of the world and with the time schedule Amanda had no choice but to keep.

Saying that Suzie cooked was an exaggeration. Amanda sighed. She knew that her daughter needed to acquire more skills, but how? Suzie was content knowing how to heat up leftovers in the microwave and to boil ramen noodles. No matter how often Amanda tried to tell her daughter that there was little to no nutrition in those processed, curly noodles, it was one of the few things Suzie would include in her all-white diet. Amanda thought about the foods her kid would eat - noodles and certainly not whole wheat, icky noodles. French fries, the kind you heat up in the oven. White bread - the kind without any "bits" added. Boiled or baked potatoes. Dried parmesan cheese. Ketchup. Well, at least there was something with color. A broiled or stir-fried chicken breast added protein along with the occasional piece of sole. Not cod or haddock or anything else that swam in the sea, just sole.

Okay, I have to turn my brain off and get some sleep. Amanda pulled the duvet higher on her shoulder and closed her eyes.

Snick. Her head popped up. She held her neck crooked at an uncomfortable angle as her eyes tried to peer through the darkness. She knew that sound. That scraping noise came when a knife was withdrawn from the knife block on the counter. The largest butcher knife, in fact. Now what in the world would Suzie be doing with that knife?

There was a creak. Yep, the floor in front of the dishwasher. The butcher block lived on the counter by the dishwasher. But, it took a lot of weight to make that particular spot creak. Even Amanda herself didn't cause the floor to protest. Her dad and her brother, yes, and Cousin Sylvia who was pushing 250, yes. But not Suzie, who was barely one hundred ten pounds after being caught out in a rain deluge.

Where her thoughts were going suddenly registered on Amanda. Those noises were not from Suzie. Who was in the house? How was that possible? She'd locked the back door before coming to bed. She always did. Didn't she?

A shoe scraped along the floor, almost as if someone had not anticipated the metal edging that separated the kitchen linoleum from where the carpet began in the hall.

A door opened in the hallway. Good. He was moving away from the basement stairs and where Suzie hunched over her computer. Amanda's head returned to the pillow in relief.

But, only for a nanosecond. The footsteps were coming this way, not that there were many places to go in this house. Amanda scared herself with the way her mind worked. There was someone in their house! And here she was criticizing him for leaving her linen closet door open. Well, Suzie always did tell her she was obsessive-compulsive about doors and drawer.

But, that meant he was getting closer. Amanda grabbed the duvet and sheet carefully in one hand and slowly drew back the covers as silently as she could. For once she was grateful that she was unable to afford that soft, down quilt she'd so admired. Rubbing it with her hands in the Bed 'n Bath store, she'd known the noise it would make every time she turned over in bed. What did that matter though when you slept alone and it didn't look like that would ever change. Thankful that she had a king-sized quilt on her queen-sized bed, Amanda bumped up the quilt in the middle of the bed, hoping it might look like a body slept soundly there. Glancing at the rocker in the corner, she spied Chatty Cathy, the doll of her childhood, the doll who stood as tall as her six year old self at the time. Cathy had long hair. Maybe, just maybe, if she tucked her into the bed, Cathy would pass for a slumbering human.

How many seconds had gone by? She had to get a grip on her thoughts. She thought that things moved fast in a crisis, but it seems like minutes and minutes since she heard the linen closet door.

There. That was the shower curtain. Her obsessiveness meant that it was always pulled closed. Why? Suzie had asked once. She couldn't remember now the reason she'd given, but "Hell if I know" would have been better.

A shoe scraped on the bathroom linoleum tile. His foot must have caught on that spot in front of the sink where the tile's lifting. His? Of course it was a his. Who ever heard of a woman breaking in to someone's house? Oh, Amanda, grab your thoughts. She'd always thought of herself as practical and level-headed. Now, in an emergency, her brain allowed in all sorts of errant thoughts. Survival. That was her priority - keeping herself and Suzie safe. She pushed the thought of her vulnerable, sweet little girl out of her mind. Her bedroom was next.

The air huffed out of Suzie's lungs and her shoulders slumped over her keyboard. "Moomm." Sheesh. Her mother knew she needed to concentrate. Why was she being so noisy? "What is she doing up there? She knows I'm trying to work. What was all that about respect and consideration for others? What time is it anyway?" Suzie glanced at the clock at the bottom of her computer screen. Almost four in the morning. Her mother should be asleep at this time of night; she was not a night owl like her. In fact, her mom was a bear when she didn't get enough sleep.

There was that banging again. Was she cleaning house at this time of the night? Suzie debated going upstairs to check, but if she did that and her mom was indeed cleaning, she might try to rope Suzie into helping. And nope, she wanted no part of that. She put on her noise cancelling headphones and stared once again at her screen. Blender was an extensive program, but tricky to use. She was having trouble getting this rendering just right and she needed it to show her fellow online gamers in tomorrow's

WAN party.

"Ugh. What was that? Even these high-end headphones couldn't dull those noises. What is mom doing?" Her face set and shoulders hunched, Suzie started up the stairs in her stocking feet.

Halfway up, she paused. There were no lights. Why would her mother clean house in the dark? Suzie proceeded slowly, avoiding the center of the third step where she knew it creaked.

Weird. The kitchen was still and silent, all tidied away for the night the way her anal mother insisted. She refused to go to bed with dirty dishes in the sink. How often had Suzie got it because she'd made herself a snack after her mom headed to bed and forgot to clean up? Sheesh, she was busy. When she got wrapped up in a tricky problem on her computer, everything else faded away. And who cared about a few dishes on the stove or counter anyway?

Something wasn't right – something was really wrong. A shoe flew out the door of her mother's bedroom and hit the wall on the other side of the hall. Her mother would never, ever treat her shoes like that. She was always lecturing Suzie that shoes cost money; don't ruin the backs, and put them away so you'll know where to find them next time.

Then she heard it; her hearing was acute. That low-pitched humming. That could not be her mother. Who was it? And that tap, tapping from her mom's room.

Suzie scrunched down the kitchen wall, resting on her haunches with her elbows welded to her sides, her head on her knees. Shutting her eyes, she concentrated on nothing but the sounds. There was no more thumping, but something was wrong. Was her mother in trouble? No, she was strong, always the one with the answers, the one who took care of them.

Suzie raised her head. In front of her line of vision was the dishwasher, slightly ajar. She knew she'd hear from her mom tomorrow about that. "Just shut the thing, Suzie. Why can't you do that?" And, the cutlery drawer was open as well. Why would that be? For sure her mom would never leave it open those few inches and Suzie had not been in the kitchen since her mom had made her come up and eat supper at the table with her. Eyes back to the dishwasher, Suzie spied the butcher block where they stored their knives. One was missing, the biggest one, the one Suzie never liked to touch because it was too sharp.

Her vision flitted rapidly around the room looking for any other abnormalities. Everything else looked in place.

The low hum resumed. That had to be a man's voice. Looking down the door, she saw her mother's bedroom door ajar. Her mom always slept with her door shut, said that Suzie moving around in the middle of the night kept her awake and she needed her sleep if she was to bring in the paycheck to support them. As long as she had her sleep, she could look after them.

Slowly Suzie unfurled herself until she was crouching. She moved to her hands and knees and crept ever so slowly down the hallway until she could peek around the open door to her mom's room. A man! He was facing the closet, grabbing at clothes and moving one hand up and down. Her mom's clothing, her good stuff that she took such pride in, was in tatters, rags of material hanging down, on the floor and wrapped around shoes and junk on the floor. And the smell. It was worse than walking by the perfume department at Sears. Suzie's head swam from the scent. Underneath that was the smell of body odor, not like her own shirt when she'd worn it too long without showering, but worse. Sort of goat-like, or what she imagined a nasty billy goat would smell like.

She retreated backwards down the hall silently and returned to her crouching against the kitchen wall. She hugged herself and rocked back and forth. She fisted her hands on her knees and beat her forehead on her entwined thumbs. Oh, this was bad, really bad. Where was her mom when she needed her?

Mom! Where was she? Had the guy got to her? She could not be hiding in the closet or he would have slashed her along with the clothes. Did she sleep through all this? Sometimes her mom wore ear plugs to bed, especially when she was in a mood to complain about Suzie's nocturnal noises.

There was a momentary pause from the bedroom. Every muscle and orifice in Suzie's body clenched. What if he came after her now? If he left the bedroom he'd see her sitting here in a ball.

She unwound and crawled back to the basement stairs, drawing the door closed behind her. There. Now he'd never know she'd been here. Silently, skipping the creaky places, Suzie retreated back to the basement, back to her safe place where she was in control, a master of her environment. She donned her headphones and pulled down the mouth piece.

The footsteps paused outside of Suzie's door now. Thank god her daughter was such a computer geek and doing her usual hibernate in the dark in the basement thing. The way the wall angled, from the top of the basement stairs, even the faint glow of the computer monitor would not be seen. And, because of her noise sensitivity, Suzie had a keyboard that was almost silent. Almost. Suzie would be wearing her noise-cancelling headphones, of course. Even with only the two of them living here and Amanda certainly didn't lead a rowdy life, Suzie insisted that she could hear the television on low one floor above or that she could hear her mother chewing popcorn as she watched a movie. So, those bulky headphones perched on her head most of the time. They would prevent Suzie from hearing that there'd been a break-in and she'd remain safely downstairs out of harm's way. Although Amanda had cursed Suzie's obsessive-compulsive streak more times than she could count, she blessed it now. Suzie's everything-in-its-place bedroom made it look like a seldom-used guest room. The intruder would think it was unused. That left just one more room for him to inspect, hers.

Hide. She had what, maybe three seconds before he made it this way. Her head swiveled, eyes scanning for the likely spots. She snatched up the mini-LED flashlight she kept by her bed. Its light was intense and she had bought it for its weight and compact size. Now, she wished for the days when she had that bulky, long flashlight that resembled a billy club.

Her closet was out; the door squeaked. She kept forgetting to oil those hinges, even though Suzie complained bitterly that the sound made her ears cramp. She was too big to fit inside the antique trunk without first removing all the accumulated junk. The wooden rocker was gorgeous and comfy but offered no hiding place. That left the bed she'd just left. Warily, she eyed it. When did they start making mattresses so close to the ground?

Her feet took her to the side farthest from the door. She lay on her stomach and inched her feet under the bed. That worked until her hips reached the edge. No go. She eased out again and flipped over onto her back. Wiggling back under, she used her elbows for purchase. This time when her hips stuck, she braced her upper arms on the floor and lifted the edge of the box spring with her hands. Only the edge of mattress was firm, she remembered. The inside was covered by just some flimsy material that had already torn when she'd gotten the vacuum nozzle stuck there some years ago. Thank god for the carpet to dull the noises she was making.

Turning her head to the side, she was under. The dust under here was incredible. When had she last vacuumed? Sure, she stuck the nozzle under here every week. Well, every few weeks, but had she ever actually moved the bed to give a good cleaning? This coming weekend, she promised herself. Yes, she would live through this and become a better housekeeper.

Good thing she was right side up. If her nose had been pressed to the carpet, she was sure she'd be sneezing.

But, how long could she stay like this? Not long with that slat pressing into her left boob. She had to move and do it now. She inch-wormed her way just a few more inches until her nose had space to breathe and no parts of her anatomy were unduly flattened. Except her stomach. Luckily that part of her was soft and posed little resistance to the box spring's support structure. Taking stock of herself, she realized that her stomach stuck out more than her boobs. That probably wasn't right. When had that happened? Another thing to begin work on next weekend.

Her ears picked up the tiny sound of her doorknob rotating in its cylinder. She turned her head. Softly, slowly, the door gently scraped the carpet in a wide arc. Amanda could see the edges of scruffy Nikes with the emblem on the side.

Pushing her cheek into the floor more, she glimpsed his silhouette as he advanced into the room. The glow from the moonlight coming in her open curtains helped. Or, not. The sheen glinted off the upheld butcher knife, the one kept so shiny and fine-edged by the built-in sharpener. Amanda's eyes closed and her lips sealed against that tiny whimper that wanted to escape.

Tap, tap, tap. A pause, then, tap-tap, tap-tap as his steps stopped. His Nikes swiveled in place, aiming towards her bed, lingering, and then moving toward the window. The tapping stopped.

Tensing her stomach to hold her insides from shivering, Amanda's gaze followed his path. She saw his heels leave the floor as he leaned into the deep windowsill, checking out her backyard. The bright slice of moon would show him that it was empty. She took in a few breaths, as deeply as she could without making noise. *I'd better fill my lungs now while I have the chance in case I need to hold my breath in a minute.*

Slowly, slowly, the scuffed shoes turned. They turned her way. The tap, tap resumed. *Was he peering at the bed? Estimating the size and shape of her body? The best place to strike first?*

Every nerve in body seized. Petrified wood had nothing on her. She willed even the blood in her veins to hold still. His toes pointed her way.

Amanda's acute hearing picked up the slightest squeak as the shoe leather protested the shifting of his weight. Now, he was so close, she could spit on his toe, right there where the leather was worn right away. But spitting required spit and her mouth was as parched as the dust bunnies living under this bed.

His clothes rustled the sound of denim on denim. Suddenly, more light penetrated Amanda's sanctuary. The bed covers had been thrown back. She felt actual pain as her heart tried to beat its panicked way through its pericardial sack, aiming for a flight path to safety out her ribs, muscles and skin.

Now. Now he knew there was no slumbering innocent in that bed. From the rumpled covers, he would know that there must have been, especially given the pristine condition of the other bedroom. Amanda again gave thanks for her daughter's excessive tidiness.

The duvet fell back into place, leaving less light for her, but still enough. Her inner child wished that the covers had enveloped her in complete darkness. Maybe if she shut her eyes, it would all go away. Maybe....

The shoes turned away and stopped. The room was only ten by eight, not much space to store objects big enough to hide in.

Her intruder again pointed his shoes toward the bed and paused. The silence pressed on her chest more heavily than the bed slats. He paused and paused. Like her, did he assume that modern day beds were built too low to the ground to provide a hiding place for anyone other than a small child? If he looked at the clothes thrown over the back of the rocking chair and the old runners tossed in the corner, he'd know that this was no child's room. Besides, no one would leave a child home alone and he already knew that the rest of the rooms were deserted.

Faintly, then more and more discernibly, the tapping resumed. Along with it came a humming. The sound was low, almost more a growl than anything melodious. Was he trying to hum a tune? Good grief, a tone-deaf assailant. Amanda winced. What was wrong with her brain? At a time like this, she'd criticize someone's musical ability? She was not that hot herself. It had been years and years since she'd touched her tenor sax, the one stored in the farthest corner of her closet. She'd given it up when Suzie was just young. No matter how sweetly Amanda would try to play, little Suzie howled at the sound and held her ears. Another one of the things that had to be sacrificed to keep her daughter content. That stirring of resentment rumbled from her stomach to the bottom of her esophagus, where she firmly tamped it down. Again. Would she have the chance to get back into her music? Her mind brought up a picture of the sax case. It was in behind her winter coat and the one floor-length dress she owned. That end of the closet was never touched.

Until now. While her thoughts flew all over the place, her intruder's shoes led him firmly to the door of her closet. Silence. Both the tapping and the weird humming stopped. Why in the world would she feel that his noises were more reassuring than his silence?

The tiny click of the latch came next, rapidly followed by the squeaking hinges as he slowly eased, then flung open the closet door. Silence for a second. He must be peering at her jumble of clothes. Then, the snick as plastic and old metal hangers slid along the pole. He pushed them one way, and then the other, moving them in bunches, looking, looking for someone - for her.

"Come out, come out, wherever you are." Then a low growl. There was a tearing sound as his knife, really her knife, raked at the clothes. Her good clothes. Did he have any idea how many hours she had spent scouring the second hand stores to acquire such a good wardrobe? No one at work ever guessed where she got her outfits. Now, they were being ruined.

Amanda felt something else stirring in her gut. This time, it went beyond resentment. How dare he? How dare this stranger enter her home, terrorize her, and then destroy her clothing? Her fists tightened against her side; her toes clenched. She was powerless to defend herself, defend her home. Why, oh why, had she chosen to cower under the bed? She was wedged like gherkins in a sealed jar. It would take her minutes to worm her way out, then what?

How long until he realized that no one was lurking in that closet? When he next turned around where would he look next? Was there an option but under the bed? Maybe he'd think she was cringing behind the couch. Right. In the dark, with the television off? Where else could she be?

Oh, god, no. The basement. That was the only place he had not searched. Oh,Suzie. How would she get to her in time? How could she protect her daughter? Leap on the guy's back as he started down the basement? It wasn't much of a plan, but it was something. Yes, she could do it. She might break both their necks in the effort, but at least she would save her little girl. Suzie had never done anything to anyone, never had the opportunity. She deserved her chance. Yes, at all costs, she must protect her child.

The sound of his escalated breathing penetrated Amanda's brain. It was rapid, noisy and wheezy, as if fragments of her tattled, knifed clothing had floated up his nose, clogging his sinuses. Good let him suffocate himself. Death by polyester and flame retardants.

Her thoughts were like herded cats, scattering, going their own way, with no cohesiveness at the time when she needed it most. Think Amanda, think. What will you do when he checks under the bed?

Her clenching fingers brushed something chilly and firm. The giddy part of her mind assured her that no part of her body was firm, so it must be something else. She scrunched one shoulder lower to lengthen her reach. There, her fingers brushed it again. Slithering an inch farther, her baby finger snagged it. Her flashlight. Her four-inch long, LED flashlight. Well, it shone brightly, so maybe she could flick it into his eyes, momentarily blinding him while she made a dash to get out from under the bed. Dash. Right. If she made it from under the bed, then she'd be parrying his knife thrusts with her mighty four inch flashlight.

His breathing, if anything, was heavier now. The knife no longer slashed, but beat against his pant leg. Next, he tossed out random shoes from the assortment on the closet floor. One hit the rocker and set it in motion. Another pinged off her dresser mirror, knocking off her only bottle of decent perfume. The heavy cut glass bottle hit the side of the dresser, and then made a soft thud when it hit the floor. Oh, no. Did I tighten the lid, Amanda wondered. The nebulizer didn't work right anymore and she took it off to dab the upended bottle on herself when she wanted to feel especially pretty. It had been months since she'd last used it. Nope, there it was. The sweet, floral, almost musky smell hit the air. If it penetrated her hidey hole under the bed, what must it smell like in the rest of the room? God, how had she ever liked it? The stench was cloying. Would the stink make him madder?

Yes, the remaining shoes came faster now; luckily she didn't have all that many. Thud. One landed partially under the bed with a crack. Oh, Amanda shuddered. Her only good pair of heels had now become flats, the spiked heel separated from the sole.

Wait. That was a gift. It was within reach. He was occupied with destroying her things and might not hear any little sound she made as she reached for the broken shoe heel, her only real weapon. But grasping it meant inching even closer to him.

Got it! She cradled the heel to her neck, experimenting with the best way to grip it in her fist. Then, the largest thud yet. It crashed into the edge of the bed, perched for a moment, then toppled to the carpeted floor, with tinny echoes. Her saxophone. The case was meant to take some abuse, but this much? Her teeth clenched and her slippery grip squeezed on the heel. Just because she hadn't touched the instrument in almost twenty years didn't mean she didn't cherish it. Nothing was sacred to this monster.

Now he was pulling every box and piece of toot she had stored on the closet's top shelf. She hoped something from the uneven stacks would clunk him on the head. Or, he would suffocate in the dust. Oh, her photo albums. All those old pictures she'd meant to secure in the album, sorting and labelling and dating... Oh, there they went. Old black and white glossies all over the floor, mixed with baby pictures of sweet Suzie, her beautiful, perfect baby.

Thoughts of Suzie filled her mind, unaware and all alone in the basement. The most vulnerable, innocent person Amanda knew. Her eyes grew hard, her face set. She would do anything to protect herself and her child. She checked for the heel in her one hand and the flashlight on the floor by her side. No!

Where was that flashlight? She must have set it down when she reached for the heel. Carefully, slowly, quietly, she tried to pass the heel across her neck to her other side. She raised her right arm slightly off the carpet and swept it from her side up to her neck to grasp the heel. She really did need to work out more. Supporting her arm inches off the floor was not as easy as one might think. There. She had it and a weapon was better in her right hand anyway. Now, her left felt along her side until her fingers crooked around the mini-light, with her thumb on the bottom button, ready to push.

Silence. Shoes shuffling on the carpet. Then that awful humming again. The sweep of his sneakers on the carpet as he circled around the end of the bed. Then he came to the side, the side farthest from where Amanda lay, as ready as she'd ever be.

The humming was replaced by grunts. Low, guttural, pigs-at-the-trough-like grunts. What was he doing? Punching her bed? Did he not know she wasn't there? Why punch the covers? Feathers floated along the edge of the bed, sprinkling the carpet with down. The knife. He was slashing her bed with her butcher knife.

Amanda shivered. She knew his intent. She'd have to act fast, catch him by surprise. Surely she could get out from under the bed fast. There was no need for stealth and she knew that she'd need to lift it off herself. She did it once, she could do it again when her life and that of Suzie's depended on it.

The slashing punches stopped. The toes remained pointed towards her while his breath heaved. Knifing a bed must be hard work, Amanda's errant brain decided.

Obviously, there was no other place in the room a person could hide. Any second now he'd look underneath the bed and find her. She had to be prepared to move. Her bare feet pinned to the floor for purchase and her fists pressed against the box spring slats. This was it.

Was his breathing slowing just a little? Amanda felt that she could hear his heart beating, her senses were so acute. He took a shuffling step back from the bed. One knee pressed to the carpet. Then, the hand with the knife rested on the floor near the edge of the bed. Should she try to make a grab for it? No, too far. She'd eased herself to the side farthest from him. Plus, what good would grabbing the blade do?

Now his forearm rested on the floor as well. She could see the sweat-stained pits of his raggedy shirt. Her nose registered his b.o., even over top of the perfume. Then one eye, a nose, mouth and part of a second eye peered at her. His lips formed something that might be mistaken for a grin if you were part of the walking dead.

"Hello," his gravelly voice said. "Ready for some fun?"

Amanda pushed with her heels to lift her butt off the floor and pushed with her palms to give her room to move. Her breath came in pants. Push, wiggle, push, wiggle. Harder, harder! Almost there. She paused for a millisecond to catch her breath. He'd be waiting for her. She had to go into attack mode instantly. Push, wiggle, push....

His hand snaked under the bed towards her. A clammy palm wrapped around her ankle. She shrieked. She couldn't help herself and couldn't spare the breath, but it came out anyway. She wiggled and pushed and squirmed with all that she had. His sweaty hand tried to hold on but lost its grip.

Next his other hand swept under the bed, the one with the knife. The moonlight caught its reflection, helping her to see where it was. That didn't help a whole lot when she had so little room to escape the blade's sweeping arc. A burn down her arm felt like when hot grease spit at her when she fried chicken in too much of a hurry. The pain in her arm reminded her of her flashlight. Before her conscious mind reasoned out the steps, her thumb depressed the switch and the tiny beam pierced the gloom, right into his eyes.

The slashing stopped and his head jerked back with a start. Next, there was a thud as something hard connected with something smashable, then his body dropped to the carpet. He lay flat and still, his eyes closed. Amanda held her breath. The only time she'd heard a sound like that was when she was a child visiting her grandparents' farm. She and her cousins had snuck into the garden. They'd pulled melons and pumpkins off their vines, lifting each one over their heads, and then smashing them to the ground.

Amanda froze, her breath caught in her closed throat. Then, a pair of tube sock feet showed near the end of the bed. The toes wiggled, the left instep riding over top of the toes on the right foot. She knew that stance.

"You can come out now," a small voice said.

CHAPTER 13

"Suzie? Suzie! Run! Quick you've got to get out of here. There's a man with a knife. Run!"

"I know, mom, I got him. You can come out now."

"You got him?" Amanda's push/wiggle routine began again with a vengeance. Almost out.

Suzie came around the side of the bed and watched her mother worm her way out. "How'd you do that?" she asked.

Amanda grabbed her daughter's arm and pulled her from the room. She glanced back over her shoulder at the body on the floor. It didn't move.

"Quick, we've got to get out of here before he comes to. What did you hit him with?"

As her mother pulled her along the hallway, Suzie held up the bat dangling from her hand. "Dad's Louisville Slugger, the one signed by some old guy from the Dodgers."

"Where'd you...."

The kitchen door flew open. Amanda pushed Suzie behind her. Men and women in uniforms raced in.

"Are you all right ma'am?" The officer took their arms and pulled Amanda and Suzie through the kitchen and out the back door where a policewoman waited. She escorted them to a police car. "You'll be safe here. Two of us will stand guard."

Amanda sank into the seat, leaning her head back and closing her eyes. Now that the immediate danger was over she felt boneless and weak. How had she ever thought she'd have the strength to take on an assailant?

But, wait. Isn't that what Suzie just did? Suzie, her Suzie? She'd actually slugged that guy and likely saved her mother's life. She reached over to fold Suzie into her arms. Even though Suzie didn't like being touched, this was one time she'd need to suck it up. Her daughter had saved her.

"But, how did you know I was in trouble? And how'd the police get here?"

"Your daughter called us, Ms. Raymore. She called 911 after spying the intruder in your room."

Amanda looked at her daughter. Her timid, anxious daughter. Suzie looked at no one. In the distance, sirens approached.

The office continued, "You should be very proud of this young woman. She has courage and keeps her cool under pressure. If she had screamed or entered the bedroom during the attack, this night might have ended very differently." She reached through the open door into the back seat. "Mind if I take this?" she asked Suzie as she reached for the baseball bat. "We'll need it for evidence." Suzie loosened her grip and allowed the officer's plastic-wrapped hand to take it and place the bat into an oversize plastic evidence bag.

They watched as an ambulance pulled into the driveway. Soon, two attendants came out carrying a gurney with a body strapped on. Amanda could make out one scruffy sneaker poking out from the hastily thrown on blanket. The attendants didn't seem to be handling their victim too gently.

"Is he, is he alive?" Amanda asked.

"I think so ma'am, but let me check." She moved away a few steps and spoke into her shoulder mike. Shortly she returned with news. "Yes, the suspect is alive but unconscious. Luckily for both of you, your daughter has a good swing and decent aim. The blow took him down, but he might not have stayed out for much longer. You never know. We wanted to get you out of the house just in case."

"It smells funny in here. I don't like it." Suzie sat forward, her knee pistoning up and down, her shoulders hunched and that vigilant look on her face as her head swiveled side to side as she rocked back and forth.

Now that Suzie mentioned it, Amanda could smell the sour odor in the back seat. She sat upright. How many greasy heads had rubbed against the back of the seat just like hers? The strobing lights of the police cars illuminated the stained seat where her daughter perched. Her yard was awash in high beams and arcing lights, the static of communication devices.

Suzie's agitation rose. She wrapped her arms tightly around herself as she rocked, eyes wide.

Exactly like a deer in headlights, Amanda thought. "Excuse me, could you turn off the roof lights on this car? They're disturbing my daughter."

"Oh, sorry, sure. They bug me, too." The strobing stopped, at least on this vehicle. "I'm just waiting for the all-clear to say we can take you back inside. The crime-scene techs are working from the outside of your house in. We're pretty sure he came in the kitchen door, but need to trace his path through the building."

"I can help you with that," offered Amanda. She had the officer's full attention. He was in the kitchen first, then he opened the basement door, I think to listen, but he didn't go down there. He took my knife from the block on the counter by the dishwasher, and then came down the hall. He went in the bathroom and I heard him open the shower curtains, then he looked in Suzie's bedroom but didn't go in. Her door was open. Then he came to my room." Amanda's voice broke on the last word. She put an arm around Suzie and drew her to her. Suzie tolerated it for just a few seconds, and then broke free to resume her rocking.

"Is there a place in your house we could take you, someplace where he didn't walk?"

Suzie spoke up. "The basement. That's where I was and he didn't come down there."

As they exited the car, Amanda took in the fresher nighttime air. A thoughtful officer brought over blankets, wrapping first Suzie then Amanda in the scratchy warmth. Suzie gripped an edge in each hand and pulled the material tight around her shoulders. Good. The pressure would help to calm her.

As they entered the back door, Amanda's gaze caught the scratches on the door striker. Noticing her stare, the policeman guarding the entryway asked if those marks had been there before. Amanda shook her head no. "I heard some scratches but I thought I was dreaming."

As they entered through the kitchen, Amanda averted her eyes from the counter where her knives made their home. She knew that barren slot would haunt her forever. She'd need new knives or could she run a home without any sharp knives? She'd certainly give it a try.

One policeman stood guarding the hallway, another shepherded them toward the stairs, while a third stood reassuringly at the bottom. "All clear, folks. We've checked this area thoroughly and there's no one here but us chickens."

"Hank!" A policewoman hollered. "Geez."

Hank blushed. "Sorry. Didn't mean anything by it - just an expression, you know. I was trying to lighten the situation after what you ladies have been through. I didn't mean that you're chicken. You..."

"Hank, can it." He did. Suzie walked by him without a glance, but Amanda managed a half smile for his efforts. "Thanks for trying," she told him.

Suzie headed for her computer, sat down and started to place her headphones on her head, her usual basement routine. An officer cleared his throat. "Ah, if we could have you sit here on the couch, we'd like to question you about what happened."

Suzie didn't hear. Her focus was on her screen and her fingers flew over the keyboard.

The police personnel as one turned from Suzie to her mother. Amanda shrugged. "She's been through a lot," she said. "Give her a few minutes to regroup. Can't you start with me?"

"It's our practice to interview each victim separately."

"Well, you are. Suzie can't hear anything we say when she has those padded headphones covering her ears. She'll be zoned out in her computer programming and not pay any attention to us."

"She wants to work at a time like this?"

"For her, this is calming and she needs it. Look, my daughter has Asperger's Syndrome, a form of autism. She feels things differently than us and computer coding is her way of relaxing. If she does that for a while, it'll give her system time to calm down and she can begin to process what happened. This was a big deal for her, if you only knew just how big." She paused then, marveling to herself, "She saved my life."

The older officer pulled out a pad and pen. Then he placed a mini recorder on the coffee table. "Do I have your permission to record this interview?? Amanda nodded. "Okay, ma'am, let's get started. For the record, please state your full name." Amanda complied.

"How many people were in this house and who normally resides here?" Amanda explained that it had been just her and Suzie since Suzie's dad left them years ago.

"What would a typical evening look like for the two of you?"

Amanda felt that their lives sounded pitiful as she explained coming home from work, putting away the groceries, making and eating supper, watching a bit of television then retiring early to bed to read then sleep. She felt like explaining that she really meant to get a life, honestly, as soon as she had a minute to figure out what that should look like and how to go about it.

"And what was your daughter doing during this time?"

Amanda nodded in Suzie's direction. "Pretty much what she's doing now. Sometimes she plays online games but she's usually in front of her computer."

"What does she do during the day? Is she employed?"

Amanda squirmed. "You have to understand. Suzie has Asperger's."

"So you said."

"Well, that makes it difficult for her, life's difficult. She's not like other young women."

"You're saying that she stays home and keeps house for you while you're away at work."

"Something like that." Amanda studied her clasped hands while the others watched Suzie's fingers flying over the keyboard.

Nodding at the computer, one officer said, "She's good. Can you imagine how my reports would get written if I had even half that speed?"

"Never in your dreams could you type like that." The others laughed then all eyes returned to Amanda.

"That gives us some background into what normal is like for you. Now please walk us through what happened tonight. I know this is hard, so take your time."

Amanda launched into her account of waking up, thinking the noises she heard were made by Suzie. Suzie often stayed up much of the night, making herself something to snack on, then returning to her computer in the basement. Amanda kept her bedroom door shut so she could sleep undisturbed when Suzie roamed around.

"But Suzie doesn't cook, apart from reheating leftovers or warming frozen food in the oven. And, no matter how many times I nag her, she is terrible about putting her dirty dishes in the dishwasher. I heard the floor creak in front of the dishwasher. A few years ago, a hose broke and the dishwasher overflowed, flooding the floor. I guess it had been leaking for a while and we didn't notice, but the floor boards in front of the dishwasher got sodden and soft. The floor's squeaked there ever since. Suzie hardly goes near the dishwasher so I was surprised when I heard that squeak. Then I heard the knife being removed from the butcher block. That's something else Suzie wouldn't do; I'm the only one who uses those knives and the largest one, the butcher knife is not used that often. The block they're stored in has a built-in sharpener for each slot, so when a knife's removed, it makes this snick sort of sound. There's nothing else in the kitchen that sounds like that. I don't think I'll ever forget that sound." The last was said almost to herself.

Amanda talked about her fears for her daughter and the relief that he'd just opened the basement door, and then shut it again. "He probably could not see the glow from her computer monitor. See?" She pointed back toward the stairs and the wall that blocked their view from the stairwell. She described the sounds of the man's incursion down the hall, opening and closing the linen closet, entering the bathroom, the scraping sound the shower curtains made as he drew them across the rod, his pause at Suzie's open bedroom door, then moving on to her room.

"Why do you think he didn't enter your daughter's room?"

"One glance probably made him think that it was a guest room that no one used. Suzie keeps it immaculately." Everyone glanced around the basement, especially the vicinity of the computer desk. That area was anything but immaculate. "I know, I know. There's a real difference in how she keeps her bedroom compared to this, the place where she spends the most time. She says she can't sleep unless everything is exactly where it's supposed to be. Even her bed covers are tight and straight."

"I know the rest is painful, but take your time and tell us as best you can what happened next. You're doing great."

Taking a big breath, Amanda started in, twisting her hands together as she relived her terror, the strange turns her mind had taken and deciding that hiding under the bed was the only thing she could do. When she talked about the tight fit and needed to lift up the mattress to slide under it, the policewoman patted her own hips saying, "Good thing you're not my size or you would never have fit." Amanda raised grateful eyes to the woman, thanking her for her sympathy and recognition that their bodies might not be what they once were.

Her voice changed when she recalled watching the destruction of her clothes. She told them how money was tight and the time she'd spent at thrift and consignment stores, trying to amass a wardrobe fit for work that fit her shoestring budget. The worst was her shoes. She only had one really good pair, saved for those most special occasions when she needed heels. And, he's ruined them - tossed those shoes around like they meant nothing. How dare he? How dare he invade her home, terrify her, threaten the lives of her and her daughter, and then destroy the only pair of really good shoes she owned?

But that broken heel flying her way had given her a weapon. Oh, she'd forgotten about her flashlight, so she mentioned picking it up off her nightstand, hoping it was at least something she could use. Then she got that heel, so she had something in each hand.

"I like your spirit. Oops, sorry. Didn't mean to interrupt. Please go ahead."

Amanda talked about the tapping of the knife, that sound ingrained in her mind, that tap, tap, tapping against his thigh. "I thought, I thought he was going to...." She looked down, blinked rapidly and couldn't finish.

"That's okay. You're doing great. Take a deep breath and take your time. We're here and we've got all night."

Amanda glanced at Suzie. She was still engrossed in her computer screen. "Well, he stopped slashing my clothes and throwing my stuff out of the closet. One of the last things he tossed was my saxophone. My sax! I have to check, to see if it's all right." She started to rise.

A hand on her shoulder gently pressed her back into the couch. "There will be plenty of time for that later. Right now your bedroom is a crime scene, so we'll let the techs do their job. They need to collect all the evidence they can. It will be a while before we can let you back into your room. You're safe right here. We'll bring you your saxophone as soon as we can."

Amanda relaxed back into the cushions. "It's not like I play it anymore anyway. Still, I might someday." She received an encouraging nod.

"The rest I don't really know. He left the closet and came to the bed, still doing that infernal tapping with the knife. He stopped by the bed and did nothing for a few minutes, at least nothing that I could see, then" he started stabbing at the covers. I don't know if he thought I was there, or…" She shuddered. "No, he'd already looked at the bed before, I forgot to tell you that. I'd tried to muss up the covers to look like there was someone under them sleeping and I put this doll, one I'd had since I was a little girl, under the covers. She has long hair so I thought it might look like a person and if this guy was just out to rob us, he might think it was someone sleeping and just walk on by." She was babbling, she was sure of it. She waited a minute to gather her thoughts before relating the very worst parts of the night.

"His shoes. You know, he should have had more respect for my good shoes because his weren't so hot. They were old and dirty and really scruffy and the one toe had the leather worn off. He stood there with his toes under the bed, so I got a good look. Too good. I won't forget them in a long time. I don't think I could ever wear a pair of Nikes now.

"It was awful while I lay there and he slashed the bed right above me. The feathers from my pillow floated down. They seemed to fall so gently when what he was doing was so violent. I was terrified that the knife would dig deep and make it all the way down to me. And I kept wondering if he knew I was there. He knew I wasn't in the closet or anywhere else in the bedroom, but someone had been sleeping in the bed. He knew the shape was just a doll. So, where else could I be? Was he playing with me? Trying to scare me? Well, it worked.

Then he stopped stabbing my bed. He just stood there. I held my breath thinking that if I didn't move, he would not know I was there. He stepped away from the bed and I thought it had worked. He was giving up; he was leaving. But then he crouched down and looked under the bed. His face was right there, just a few feet from mine and he looked at me. He looked! And he had this look on his face, I can't describe it, but he enjoyed it. He liked terrorizing me and he liked what he planned to do to me." Her voice broke and her shoulders shook. The policewoman moved to put an arm around her and pat her back. There was silence in the room.

While they focused on Amanda and her distress, no one noticed Suzie's approach.

"Maybe it should be my turn now." All eyes turned to Suzie.

"Why?" her mom asked. She was so not used to Suzie taking the initiative.

"You look like you're upset. You can take a break while they question me."

Amanda stared at her daughter. Did Suzie just demonstrate compassion for how her mother might be feeling? She so rarely took into account anyone's feelings other than her own. Amanda shook that bitter thought from her mind. Of course Suzie did the best she could; they both did. It's just that Suzie seemed so inwardly focused, so immersed in her own thoughts and interests that the wants or needs of others didn't seem to enter the equation. But now Suzie showed caring for her mother. Was she actually trying to offer comfort? She squeezed her daughter's hand. Suzie tolerated it for a second, and then pulled away, wrapping her arms around herself.

The officer who led the questioning turned to Amanda. "It's policy that we question witnesses separately. We made an exception because your daughter couldn't hear your interview with her headphones on. May I ask if you'd step back outside and wait with Constable Barlow here?" He nodded at the woman whose arm was still around Amanda's shoulders.

Amanda was startled. "No. No, I can't possibly leave Suzie alone. You don't understand. She's been through a lot, we both have, but she's too young to be questioned without a parent present."

"How old are you, miss?" he asked.

Without meeting his gaze, Suzie's small voice said, "Twenty-one."

Turning back to Amanda, "That's several years over the age of consent. She's an adult. We're on solid legal ground to question her alone."

"But she has trouble with strangers. She doesn't like to talk to people; I have to do a lot of her speaking for her, especially when she doesn't know someone. She's anxious. She might get overwhelmed. She…"

"Mom."

"No, it's out of the question. She'll need my help to get through anything else tonight and..."

Louder, "Mom." When she had Amanda's attention, Suzie continued. "I'll be all right. Go, go wait outside. The sooner you go, the sooner this will be over and it can be just us again."

Amanda wished she could get a good look at her daughter's face, but Suzie studied the digital face of her atomic watch.

"Are you sure?"

"Mom, I just told you. Didn't you listen? Are you having auditory processing problems?"

"Okay, okay. Look, I'll be just in the backyard with..."

"Constable Barlow," Suzie supplied.

"Yes, Constable Barlow." She rose but stood reluctantly, clearly uneasy about leaving Suzie on her own with these policemen. "Just call if you need me and I'll be right here." She glared at the interrogating officer. "If you do anything to upset her...."

He threw up his hands in a defensive position. "Honest, we'll be gentle. We don't want to put her through anything more than we have to after all she's experienced tonight. But we do need to get her statement. We want to nail this guy and both your testimonies will be needed."

He waited until Amanda and Constable Barlow went up the stairs before turning back to Suzie. "Would you have a seat, please?"

"No."

"No? Come on over here; you'll be more comfortable sitting on this couch."

"No." Then a second later, "Thank you."

"Is there somewhere else you'd rather sit?"

"No."

"Is there someplace better to do this interview?"

"No."

"Then where do you want to go?"

"Here." Suzie walked to the other side of the coffee table and took four steps. The officer started to follow her, but she abruptly turned around, almost walking into him. He back peddled, and Suzie took two more steps, then turned and paced back the way she had come. Four steps, spin, four steps, over and over while the policemen watched. One cleared his throat.

Suzie glanced up at him briefly, then down again, never breaking her pacing. Minutes went by. Still watching the path her feet wore in the shag carpet, Suzie said, "Is this how you questioned my mother? I thought you only sweated confessions out of hostile witnesses. I saw that on TV."

"We were waiting for you to sit down before we began."

"I'm not sitting. Didn't we already go over that?"

"Right. We, um thought you were pacing for a minute then would sit down and we'd begin."

"I've been pacing for exactly four and three quarters minutes. That's longer than a minute."

"We can start whenever you're ready. If you'd like to have a seat now...."

"I said I was not sitting. Do you find multi-tasking difficult? You're talking now while you stand? Why can't I? I can talk and walk at the same time. Don't you ever do that?"

James Codwell had been in the service a long time. He'd interviewed victims and punks but never met anyone quite like Suzie. He didn't know whether to be mad, insulted or to laugh. Was she pulling his leg? She looked like such a mousey little thing, but didn't seem to have any trouble speaking her mind. "Are you saying you want us to conduct the interview like this? Do you want me to walk with you?"

Suzie's one arm gestured around the basement. "If it makes you feel better, go ahead."

"Does pacing make you feel better?"

"Why would I do it if it didn't?"

She had a point. Sergeant Codwell cleared his throat, and hovered a finger over the recorder. "You understand that we need to record this interview."

Suzie gave no indication that she'd heard.

"Ms. Fletcher, do you understand that I'm about to turn on the recorder?"

"Oh, yes. I didn't realize that was a question. You have to phrase things differently if you want people to understand that you are asking a question and expect a reply. There are grammar and syntax rules that help people communicate with one another."

"Yes, I'm aware of that. I'll be more careful." He shook his head.

"Nonverbal language conveys at least as much information as the words you say. You just shook your head. That means no. Did you shake your head because you are actually conveying that you will not be careful? Your actions don't seem careful to me."

Now he was getting ticked. "There's no reason to be a smart ass with me, young lady."

Suzie peered at him as she spun at the end of her pace line. There was no smirk or grin, no expression at all on her face. Maybe puzzlement, James thought, but she was difficult to read.

James decided to press on. "Just tell us what happened, in whichever way you want."

Suzie's pacing pattern took a turn and she headed for her computer, pulling her keyboard forward and grabbing her head phones.

"Whoa, what are you doing?"

"I'm going to tell you what happened in my own way." Her fingers began to fly over the keys.

James rose to stand beside the computer. "No, writing isn't any good. You need to tell us by talking."

"Writing is so good," retorted Suzie. "Writing is pure. It's not muddied up with facial expressions. And you can't forget it; you can come back again and again and the words are still there without worrying about memory." She spoke while she typed.

Bentley watched, fascinated. "How does she do that?" he mouthed to James.

James placed his hand over Suzie's. She froze, then pulled her hands out from under his, rubbing the backs hard against her thighs. "Don't touch me," she said. "I don't like that."

"Well, I don't like you typing right now. We're trying to conduct an interview here and you're wasting our time. Get back over and either sit down or pace, but tell us what happened. Use your words, your spoken words."

Suzie resumed her pacing. "I was doing my work. Down here, like I always do. Mom had gone to bed; she says she needs her sleep. I heard the basement door open and it made me mad. Mom knows that I don't like to be disturbed when I'm concentrating. I just need to be left alone. But she must have thought better of it because she shut the door and didn't come down. At least I thought it was mom.

"Then I started hearing these noises."

"When?" James asked. "How long after you heard the basement door close?"

"I don't know. I was in the zone, you know and the rendering was going great. Wait." She plunked down in her computer chair and started typing.

"I thought we were clear that you needed to talk, not write this out."

Suzie ignored him. She stared at the screen, paused, then typed some more. A three dimensional drawing rotated on the monitor, partially colored, partially still a line drawing. "There," she pointed to the corner of the screen. "I knew I'd saved different versions of the rendering. I saved one when I heard the door open, knowing that Mom was about to interrupt me. That was at 2:38." She typed some more and images blasted across the screen, then held still. "The next time I saved was when I heard all that banging upstairs and I knew I was going to be interrupted again. 2:46." She got up and fell into her pacing rhythm.

"There was all this banging from upstairs and it sounded like it was from mom's room. A weird time of night for her to house clean because she was always so picky about things being quiet at night because she had to sleep or she'd be no good at her job the next day. But mom says you shouldn't pigeon-hole people so I thought she was trying something different. It's good not to get stale, you know, especially when you're old like mom.

"It was really annoying because I was trying to work. Mom talks about having consideration for other people and wants me to be quiet when she's sleeping or concentrating, but she was not being very considerate of me. I could hear the racket even through these head phones and they're the best quality noise cancelling ones I could find. I should know; I researched them for months before insisting she buy me some.

"Then the noises got louder like something heavy fell. I thought Mom might call me to come help her lift something. You lose muscle mass as you age, you know and she's not young anymore so sometimes asks me to help. Sometimes even when I'm busy.

"But there was nothing. I worked a bit longer, but still she didn't yell for me to help. At first I was glad it was quiet again so I could work. Blender is a really tricky program - so comprehensive the possibilities are vast, but it can be hard to get some aspects right." She looked up at James. "It's not a program I'd suggest you try. Blender requires precision and a person who is not precise in his language may show that trait in other areas as well. No, Blender would not work for someone like you." She brightened. "But, if you want to get into rendering or digital enhancement, I could recommend something easier for you to use."

What was with this girl? Was she for real or was she pulling his leg. Deciding to take the high road, especially in the face of his smirking co-workers, James suggested Suzie get back to telling her story. "What happened next?"

"Mom says that sometimes I get too far inside my own head and that I need to come out once in a while to see what other people are doing and if I can help them. Her in particular, I think she means. She tells me that it's not all about me. I'm not self-centered, really, it's just that my work is important to me and I concentrate intensely.

"But those noises bugged me and it bugged me even more the way they just stopped. So I thought I'd go see. Just in case Mom had gone back to sleep, I was quiet on the stairs. When I got to the kitchen, the noises started again and I could hear stuff tearing. Why would mom be ripping stuff up? She hates messes.

"While I was thinking about this, I noticed the counter across from me. Mom always set the butcher block just so, exactly perpendicular to the wall, but this time it was off, just slightly. And the biggest knife was gone. We hardly ever use it.

"Then these quieter thuds came from Mom's bedroom and tearing sounds. I crawled down the hall to peek." Suzie shuddered and the first real expression came over her face that James had noticed. "This man. He was standing over Mom's bed, hacking at it. At first I thought he was killing my mom, but there was no blood, so I knew she wasn't in bed dead. And I could see the mess on the floor and into her closet so I knew she wasn't there. No blood anywhere. The only place to hide in her room was under the bed.

"What if he slashed right through the mattress and got her? What if he looked under the bed? He had to know she was there because her bedroom door is always shut.

"I know how to be quiet. Mom's always telling me to keep quiet and let her sleep if I must roam around all night. I don't really roam all night. It's just that my brain comes alive that time of day and I work my best but sometimes I need a snack or to use the bathroom so I have to come upstairs. I've learned how to be quiet to avoid fights with Mom."

James made a continue motion with his right hand.

Suzie stopped pacing and looked at him. "Is your hand hurting you?" she asked.

James sighed; his buddy snickered. "Please continue."

"My dad left us when I was little. He couldn't stand the thought that I was different. I'm not really different, Mom says, I'm unique. I step to the beat of my own drummer and dad was not like that. He was a joiner, a fitter-inner, wanting us to blend in. I guess I didn't do that so well when I was younger and mom supported me, so he left. The only thing I have of him is his Louisville Slugger. Dad used to play a lot of softball - part of his joiner stuff. He loved baseball and teams and groups. He had this signed bat he loved. Mom thinks he forgot, he packed so fast when he left. She kept it in case he ever came back for it. When I was little I'd see her sometimes take it out and look at it. Sometimes she'd cry when she thought I was asleep. Then she put it away, behind the furnace where we don't go very often. But I knew where it was and that it was strong. Mom says you should have seen daddy swing that bat.

"So, I swung the bat, too. I hit the guy because he was going after my mom. She was defenseless under that bed. When I got back to her bedroom, he was on the floor with one arm under the bed. His other hand rested on top of the bed and didn't have a knife in it. He meant to hurt my mom, so I hit him. He fell down and didn't move. Then I told Mom she could come out now." Then she remembered. "Oh, I was not logical. I missed a step; that is so not like me. When I went back downstairs to get the bat, I first came here to my computer. I opened up my VOIP program and called 911. The lady told me to stay on the line with her and keep talking, but that didn't make sense when Mom needed my help, so I hung up on her. My Mom is more important than following the rules, right?"

Voices came from the kitchen, raised voices, and then footsteps on the stairs. Everyone looked up as Amanda and Constable Barlow scurried down the stairs.

"Sarg, I'm sorry. I tried to keep her outside, but she insisted she had to get back to her daughter."

Amanda rushed to Suzie and grabbed her arms. "Are you all right? Are you okay?"

Suzie nodded, surprisingly calm. She pulled away from her mom's hands.

James scowled at Officer Barlow, who was supposed to keep Amanda away from the interrogation, then frowned at Amanda. "Ma'am, we were not finished interviewing your daughter. She was still recounting the events of the night."

"I know, but Suzie does not do well with strangers. She's not used to them and needs me to be here."

"Mo-o-o-m." Was Suzie embarrassed? Naw, that's not an emotion she showed. Amanda could not remember a time when she'd actually thought Suzie was embarrassed.

Amanda was in mother hen mode. After all, she'd almost lost her child tonight, and her own life as well. If ever she had the right and the need to be protective, it was now.

"She's been through enough. You can't ask her anything else without my being here. I know her and can tell when she's had too much. She's fragile, not like other people."

"Mo-o-m." Suzie's wail was more exasperated than distressed, more like that of a teenager. "I'm fine."

"No, you're not and neither am I. Nothing will ever be fine again."

Suzie's eyes widened at that.

Constable Barlow, placed a hand on Amanda's arm. "I know it feels like that right now. Everyone feels like that when bad stuff like this happens. But, things will start to feel better down the road. Honest. And, in the meantime, we have victim support counselors who can help. It takes a while to feel safe again, I know."

Amanda looked questioningly at her.

"Yes, I know both professionally and personally. And yes, I went through a home invasion, or my family did. I was at work at the time."

"Oh," was all Amanda could say.

James pointed at the couch. "If you wouldn't mind having a seat here, we'll continue with your daughter." When Amanda sat down, he turned to where Suzie still stood. At least she wasn't pacing anymore. "Is there anything else you want to tell us?"

Suzie shook her head.

"Um," came from Amanda. "You might want to rephrase that."

The officers all looked at her. Suzie watched a spot on the floor.

"Suzie takes what you say at face value. You asked her if there was anything else she wanted to say. That's a different question than asking if there is anything else she should tell you about what happened."

James looked from Amanda to Suzie, wondering which one of them was nuts. Maybe they weren't always like this; they were just addled by all they'd been through tonight.

"Ma'am, if you wish to be allowed to remain in this room while we question your daughter, you will keep quiet and not interfere. I assure you, we are experienced at this and Ms. Raymore is doing fine. She's actually an excellent witness." He went over Suzie's story several more times, probing for more details, seeking out any discrepancies. There were none. Suzie's recitation was bare bones but accurate, without the hysterics that were so common in tense situations.

After thanking Suzie, he told her she could relax for a few minutes while he reviewed a few details of her mother's story. Suzie escaped to her computer, donning her headphones and immersing herself in the world of Halo.

Shaking his head at her, he turned back to Amanda to check for any details she'd missed or anything else she needed to add. He asked for her story all over again, from the beginning.

Amanda's retelling was less tearful this time, but no less emotional. It was a stark contrast to the dispassionate way her daughter had recited the happenings of the night.

Finally, as Amanda drooped on the couch and Suzie hunched over her keyboard, James snapped his notebook shut and rose. "I think we're about done here for now. We may have more questions for you tomorrow and one of my officers will be in touch."

"You're leaving?" There was a tremor in Amanda's voice.

"I am. I need to go to the hospital to check on the suspect."

Amanda blanched. "He won't be out free, will he? What if he comes back?"

"No, he most definitely will not be walking the streets tonight. He'll either be in hospital under guard or locked up in jail."

This was reassuring, but Amanda still raised her eyes up the stairs nervously. His reassurance did little to allay her fears. They were safe for tonight then, but what about after that? How would she ever feel safe again?

"Constable Barlow will remain in the house with you for the rest of the night and I'll post one officer outside. You're safe now." He stood and straightened his uniform. "Um, can we get your daughter's attention?"

Amanda went to Suzie and squeezed her shoulder. When Suzie shoved back her headphones, Amanda took her hand and pulled her over to where the group of police officers waited.

James held out his hand first to Amanda, then to Suzie. "Thank you for your assistance. We're sorry that you had to experience something like this, but we've got the guy, thanks to you." He nodded at Suzie. "Constable Barlow will tell you how to get in touch with Victim's Services. They'll help you deal with some of this mess and they have excellent counselors on staff. I would suggest that you avail yourself of counseling services from them or some other agency; they can really help in getting over traumas like the one you've been through tonight.

"Ms. Raymore, you should be very proud of your daughter. Due to her quick thinking and actions, this night turned out much better than it could have."

"Again, I am glad that you're both all right. Ms. Raymore." He held out his hand to Amanda.

After shaking, he turned to Suzie and stuck out his hand. "Suzie."

The young woman's shoulders straightened. "My name is Suzanne."

# # #

NOTE FROM THE AUTHOR

Thank you for spending this time with Suzie and her mom. If you have enjoyed this story, the author would be greatly appreciative if you would leave a review at this link: https://www.amazon.com/Autism-Grows-School-Daze-Book-ebook/dp/B01JB8QW3U. Reviews mean a lot to authors.

Author Dr. Sharon Mitchell loves connecting with readers. Contact her through her website at http://www.drsharonmitchell.org. There you will find information on her other books her workshop appearances and questions families and teachers often ask about kids who have autism spectrum disorders.

Would you like to join the author's review team? Team members receive complimentary, advance copies of each new title. Contact Sharon at http://www.drsharonmitchell.org.

Turn the page to see the other books in the series.

Other Books in the Series

There's more! If you liked Autism Grows Up, you might also enjoy the other books in the series. Each focuses on a different child who has an autism spectrum disorder. Many of the same characters appear in each book.

Autism Goes to School

Autism Runs Away

Autism Belongs

Autism Talks & Talks

Autism Grows Up

The Autism Goes to School Workbook (coming in 2017)

Prequel to Autism Goes to School (coming in 2017)

Turn the page for a synopsis of each book and more information.

Autism Goes to School

We're thrilled to announce that this Amazon bestseller is also a B.R.A.G. Medallion winner!

To celebrate, we're offering this book to you FREE at BookHip.com/ZPHDQC.

After suddenly receiving custody of his five year old son, Ben must learn how to be a dad. The fact that he'd even fathered a child was news to him. Not only does this mean restructuring his sixty-hour workweek and becoming responsible for another human being, but also Kyle has autism.

Enter the school system and a shaky beginning. Under the guidance of a gifted teacher, Ben and Kyle take tentative steps to becoming father and son.

Teacher Melanie Nicols sees Ben as a deadbeat dad, but grudgingly comes to admire how he hangs in, determined to learn for his son's sake. Her admiration grows to more as father and son come to rely on Melanie being a part of their lives.

When parents receive the news that their child has autism, they spend countless hours researching the subject, usually at night, after an exhausting day. Teachers, when they hear that they'll have a student with an autism spectrum disorder, also try to learn as much as they can. This novel was written for such parents and teachers - an entertaining read that offers information on autism and strategies that work.

Bonus Section
At the back of the book are links and references useful to parents and teachers.

You can find Autism Goes to School FREE at these retailers:

Amazon.com
iTunes

BookHip.com/ZPHDQC
Kobo
Barnes & Noble paperback
Barnes & Noble e-book

Autism Goes to School is available FREE in all formats at BookHip.com/ZPHDQC.

What Are Reviewers Saying About Autism Goes to School?

- "A gem of a book"
- " A true delight - Highly, highly recommended
- Just couldn't put it down"
- "Highly informative and extremely helpful - Couldn't take my eyes off it"
- I loved this book from beginning to end - Just plain awesome
- I could feel the author's passion - What a great way to learn about autism
- "Entertains, entrances & educates: 3 for the price of one!"
- "This wonderful book is about a Dad, Ben, meeting his autistic son Kyle for the very first time, when Mom dumps him suddenly on his doorstep, saying she can no longer take care of him. Through the eyes of Ben, we get a glimpse of both the challenges and joys of being a parent of a child who sees the world in different ways."
- "Unlike some stories that speak of autistic children, this one brings a wealth of hope and information! As we look over Ben's shoulder, we see a glimpse of the learning tools currently being used in the classroom today, and we get glimpses of things that could be helpful in the day to day life of an autistic child."
- "I appreciated this story on several levels. First I enjoyed the story of Ben discovering what it means to be a parent, especially a single parent. Second, I enjoyed watching Kyle find his own means of success in this new and upside down world. "
- "I enjoyed the glimpse into classroom life and options available today. Finally I enjoyed the quiet romance between Mel and Ben."

Autism Runs Away

Ethan is only in grade one and already has been kicked out of one school due to his tantrums and pattern of running away when in a panic. Now, his mom's enrolled him in a new school but remains glued to her phone, waiting for the call to tell her to come pick him up, that they can't handle him, that they don't know what to do with a child who has autism.

How can she trust these strangers to look after her son, just one small child among hundreds, when he has run from own parents so very many times? They don't know the terror of losing your child in a mall or watching him run blindly into traffic.

What started as a fun chase game when Ethan was a toddler has turned into a terrifying deviation. The adults in his life never know when he might take off.

Rather than attaching an adult to his side to keep him safe, this new teacher talks about calming strategies and choices. Do they not realize what could happen if Ethan flees the building? The impact of a car on one small body? Sara is about to learn if this new school is up to the challenge.

Meet Kyle, Mel, Ben and the other characters you got to know in the Amazon bestseller Autism Goes to School. See what they've been up to in the last year and how they join forces to help Ethan.

For free sample chapters of Autism Runs Away, go to BookHip.com/QKCLG.

Get Autism Runs Away here: https://www.amazon.com/Autism-Runs-Away-Book-School-ebook/dp/B01FCYQ7DC.

Autism Belongs

Manny is not like other children. He doesn't talk. He doesn't leave the house. His parents desperately try to arrange their world so that Manny does not get upset. Because, when he does, well, the aggression was getting worse. Too many times Tomas had to leave work to rescue his wife from the havoc of their son's meltdowns. At ten, Manny was becoming difficult to handle.

Passing by a bakery made all the difference. There, they met people who understand autism, along with its strengths and challenges. They learn ways to help Manny communicate and socialize and to have his needs met.

Dare they consider letting him go to school? Is there a chance that Manny actually belongs there? You bet.

Meet Kyle, Ben, Mel and the other characters you read about in the Amazon bestseller Autism Goes to School and see how they've grown and progressed.

Free chapters of Autism Belongs are available in all formats at BookHip.com/ SGCVFJ.

You can find Autism Belongs on Amazon at this URL: https://www.amazon.com/Autism-Belongs-School-Daze-Book-ebook/dp/B0184ZQMI6/.

Autism Talks and Talks

Karen is a grade 6 student who has Asperger's Syndrome. She is bright, vivacious and highly verbal. Too verbal. She finds certain topics fascinating, studies them in-depth and is all too willing to share her knowledge with others. She goes on and on and on, not realizing that she is boring and alienating the other kids with her endless monologues. Her protective mom tries to shield her from the world, limiting her contact with peers in case she might be bullied.

Karen would like to be social. She remains on the fringe, looking at other adolescents having fun together and wondering if she could ever be a part of the group.

Karen has potential. Her inability to read body language and her lack of knowledge in social pragmatics get in the way of interacting with others her age and having friends. Through a structured group at school, she begins to understand the give and take of conversation and to have some positive experiences with her peers.

And, can a young man with Asperger's find love?

Free chapters of Autism Talks and Talks are available in all formats at BookHip.com/LTGFAB.

Get your copy of Autism Talks and Talks on Amazon at this link: https://www.amazon.com/Autism-Talks-Book-School-Daze-ebook/dp/B01IIUZH3S.

Autism Grows Up

At twenty-one, Suzie has withdrawn from a world she finds alien and confusing. Ability is not the problem, nor is interest – many things fascinate her. But, she has Asperger's Syndrome and high anxiety. To her, the world is a harsh, scary place where she does not fit.

Suzie lives with her mother, Amanda. She spends much of her day sleeping and most of her nights on the computer. Her mom wishes Suzie would get a job, go to school or at least help out around the house. Suzie feels that her time is amply filled with the compelling world lurking within her comp.

Amanda has two full time jobs – one involves working at the office every day, the second involves looking after Suzie. Amanda wants more for Suze, but does not know how to help her move forward. When she tries putting pressure on her, Suzie suffers from paralyzing anxiety, resulting in morose withdrawal or worse, lengthy tantrums. Suzie is most content when alone in the basement with her computer. Staring at her monitor, the rest of the world falls away and she feels at home.

Amanda is torn. She met this gentleman, Jack. It would be nice to spend time with someone other than her brother and daughter but Suzie wouldn't like it and she needs her mother desperately. Amanda's brother asks uncomfortable questions like what will become of Suzie if something happens to Amanda.

Jack gently persists and Amanda glimpses what her life could be like. Suzie resents the time her mom spends with Jack and makes her mother pay for the hours not devoted to her daughter.

When, they have a home invasion Amanda has only Suzie to rely on.

For free sample chapters of Autism Grows Up in all formats, head to this link: BookHip.com/ KSGVSC.

Autism Grows Up is for sale on Amazon at https://www.amazon.com/Autism-Grows-School-Daze-Book-ebook/dp/B01JB8QW3U.

Autism Goes to School Workbook

Readers who followed Ben and Kyle's journey in *Autism Goes to School* have said that they would like a guide to help them follow the strategies that Ben and Kyle try. Of course, not every strategy works for everyone. Remember that once you've met a child with autism, you have met one child with autism. While we're all unique, there is often a core cluster of characteristics that kids on the spectrum share.

The workbook looks at the things Ben did right and the mistakes he made, despite his good intentions. It looks at Kyle's responses, and then guides you to consider how your child with autism might respond.

There is space to profile your son, daughter or student's strengths and the areas that pose the most challenge right now.

The guide will help you look at the sensory issues that might contribute to the difficulties and ways to help. It discusses the communicative aspect of behavior and how you can help the child better express his wants and needs in appropriate ways. A self-regulated child is a calmer, happier child.

There are examples of visuals and schedules and space to create your own. And, there is an extensive list of references that will help you guide your child to be as independent as he can be.

The Autism Goes to School Workbook will be available on Amazon in 2017.

A free Advanced Reader Copy will be sent to everyone on the Review Team. To join the team, leave a message for Dr. Mitchell at http://www.drsharonmitchell.org.

Prequel to Autism Goes to School

Readers have asked about the lives of Jeff and Mel prior to Autism Goes to School. Coming in 2017 you can read their stories. Go along with Jeff to his first try at college and living away from home. Follow Mel's path as she learns more autism spectrum disorders. Learn about the struggles as their family struggles with the balance of protecting Jeff and fostering his independence.

This Prequel to Autism Goes to School will be out in 2017.

And, of course, you can get your FREE copy of Autism Goes to School in all formats here: BookHip.com/ZPHDQC.

ABOUT THE AUTHOR

Dr. Sharon A. Mitchell has worked as a teacher, counselor, psychologist and consultant for over thirty years. Her Master's and Doctorate degrees focused on autism spectrum disorders. She has delivered workshops and seminars to thousands of participants at regional and national conferences. Her passion is helping people with autism and those who support them.

Sharon loves connecting with readers. Contact her through her website at http://www.drsharonmitchell.org. There you will find information on her other books her workshop appearances and questions families and teachers often ask about kids who have autism spectrum disorders.

Send her a message at questions@drsharonmitchell.org if you're interested in joining her review team.

www.ingramcontent.com/pod-product-compliance
Lightning Source LLC
Chambersburg PA
CBHW070114080526
44586CB00013B/1290